THE ITALIAN-AMERICAN EXPERIENCE

An Annotated and Classified Bibliographical Guide

WITH SELECTED PUBLICATIONS OF THE
CASA ITALIANA EDUCATIONAL BUREAU

by

FRANCESCO CORDASCO
MONTCLAIR STATE COLLEGE

BURT FRANKLIN & CO.
NEW YORK

Cordasco, Francesco, 1920-
    The Italian-American experience.

    (Burt Franklin ethnic bibliographical guide 1)
    "Appendix: Casa Italiana Educational Bureau publications"; p.
    1. Italians in the United States—Bibliography. I. Title.
Z1361.I8C658   016.9173'06'51   74-10922
ISBN 0-8337-5526-9

IN MEMORY OF

Carmela Madorma Cordasco
1883-1962

Giovanni Cordasco
1883-1953

Rosina Cordasco
1878-1962

Vincenzo Cordasco
1887-1967

Palma Cordasco Caruso
1886-1924

Resolute Voyagers to the New World

TABLE OF CONTENTS

It is urged that the Italian race stock is inferior and degraded; that it will not assimilate naturally or readily with the prevailing "Anglo-Saxon" race stock of this country; that intermixture, if practicable, will be detrimental; that servility, filthy habits of life, and hopelessly degraded standard of needs and ambitions have been ingrained in the Italians by centuries of oppression and abject poverty; that they are incapable of any adequate appreciation of our free institutions and privileges and duties of citizenship; that the greater part are illiterate and likely to remain so; that they are lowering and will inevitably lower the American standard of living and labor and citizenship; that they are crowding out American laborers from avenues of employment; that their labor is no longer needed here for the development of the country; that a large percentage are paupers or on the verge of pauperism, and that the inevitable influence of their influx is pauperizing; that they make the slums in our large cities; that they burden our charitable institutions and prisons; and that there is no material evidence of progress and prospect of relief without the enforcement of wide ranging exclusion.

Eliot Lord, et al., *The Italian in America* (1905)

INTRODUCTION

INTRODUCTION

The new interest in ethnicity derives from the Civil Rights Movement of the last two decades, and the Black consciousness which accompanied it: in a very real sense, the emergence of a white ethnic consciousness (Italian, Irish, Jewish, Polish, Slavic, etc.) is to be understood as a reaction to the special "Minority" status accorded over the turbulent 1960s to Blacks, Hispanics (a rubric incongruously lumping together Puerto Ricans, Cubans [for the most part middle class political expatriates] and Mexicans); to the Johnsonian War on Poverty and the Federal interventions in behalf of the newly discovered minorities; and to the concomitant egalitarianism which was viewed as a threat to white ethnic status.[1] The new ethnic identity so vigorously affirmed by the descendents of white European immigrants had always been there, if somewhat dormant: it was catalyzed by the ethnic fever which gripped America in the 1960s.

In still another sense, ethnic identity has always been a fact of life in the United States; assimilation, as proposed in the concept of "the melting pot" never really occurred: it is this theme which Michael Novak has polemically conceptual-

---

[1]It is a cruel irony that the descendents of white European ethnics have been denied "minority" status by the formulas and identities defined (out of the "discovery" of poverty in the mid-1960s) by the bureaucratic U.S. Department of Health, Education and Welfare: if Blacks, Hispanics, Orientals and American Indians constitute the only minorities in contemporary America, this is not only false sociology but a mock conversion of Italians, Jews, Poles, Greeks and other ethnics into acceptable *Wasp* postures. In the universities and colleges, ethnics (particularly Italians), latecomers to *academia*, have found themselves the victims of "affirmative action criteria" for hiring and promotion, invidiously the adversaries of Blacks, Hispanics, Orientals, and Indians (and belatedly, women). See Paul Seabury "HEW and the Universities," *Commentary*, February 1972, pp. 38-45, and correspondence, *Ibid.*, May 1972.

i

ized, and which Peter Schrag has caustically pursued in his obsequies for the American *Wasp*.[2]

In a perspicacious review of the literature on European Americans, Rudolph J. Vecoli has observed:

> Ethnicity has exercised a persistent and pervasive influence upon American history. Americans have traditionally defined themselves and others as members of ethnocultural groups. On the basis of their origins, national, racial, religious and regional, they have shared with "their own kind" a sense of a common heritage and collective destiny. Ethnic cultures have sustained patterns of values, attitudes, and behaviors which have differentiated various segments of the population. The resulting ethnic pluralism has profoundly affected all aspects of American life. Religion, politics, social mobility, even the conduct of foreign affairs, have reflected this extraordinary diversity of ethnic identities.
>
> A series of migrations, internal as well as external, brought together peoples of various cultural, linguistic, racial and religious backgrounds. The peopling of this continent by trans-oceanic migration has gone on for over four hundred years. The original inhabitants, the true native Americans, were gradually displaced and dispossessed by successive waves of immigrants. They came from all over the world, Africans by the millions, brought to this land in chains, Asiatics by the hundreds of thousands, and others from countries to the north and south and from the islands of the Caribbean. But the vast majority came from Europe. In the greatest population movement in human history, some thirty-five million Europeans

[2]Michael Novak, *The Rise of the Unmeltable Ethnics: Politics and Culture in the Seventies* (New York: Macmillan, 1971); Peter Schrag, *The Decline of the Wasp* (New York: Simon and Schuster, 1971).

immigrated to the United States in the century
after 1830. This fact determined the basic character of American society; it was to be predominantly Caucasian, Christian and Western.[3]

There is little doubt that the "extraordinary diversity of
ethnic identities" affected all aspects of American life:
essentially, it is a belated historical revisionism which is re-
casting the corpus of American history and its institutions,
and correctly reflecting the inseparableness of ethnic identity
from the socio-historical chronicles of the American experience. Put another way, there is no American history without
its ethnic experience; equally, there is no Black history in
America outside the white sociological matrix which defines
both its parameters and responses. The attempts to translate
white ethnic proletarian struggles and Black power nationalism into full-fledged social movements are parts of the
evolving historical record; history absorbs into its canons the
totality of an age, allowing parity to all events as part of the
record: it can scarcely afford the conceptual luxuries of
sociology which transforms facts and personages into ordi-
nate and subordinate statuses, into phenomenologies and
disputants.[4]

The Italian experience in the United States has been
indescribably diverse; that its study has been neglected is in

[3]Rudolph J. Vecoli, "European Americans: From Immigrants to Ethnics,"
International Migration Review, vol. 6 (Winter 1972), p. 403.

[4]On the transformation of the Black power nationalism into a social movement, see Bayard Rustin, "From Protest to Politics," *Commentary* (February
1965); Paul Feldman, "The Pathos of Black Power," *Dissent* (January-February
1967); Tom Milstein, "Perspectives on the Panthers," *Commentary* (September
1970); and Daniel P. Moynihan "Text of Pre-Inauguration Memo to President-
elect Richard M. Nixon," *New York Times*, March 11, 1970. See also, F.
Cordasco, "Charles Loring Brace and the Dangerous Classes: Historical Analogues
of the Urban Black Poor," *Journal of Human Relations*, vol. 20 (third Quarter,
1972), pp. 379-386. The Italian-American poet, Vincent Ferrini, deals with
themes of the minority poor and their exploitation by a corrupt economic system. See Ferrini's *Blood of the Tenement* (1944); *Injunction* (1943); *The Plow in
the Ruins* (1946); *No Smoke* (1941); and *Tidal Wave of the Great Strikes* (1946).

keeping with the neglect accorded the study of other ethnic groups (an exception would be the Jewish community) but for the Italian-American the neglect of his past in America has obscured his present state and prospects: and it might be cogently argued that Italian-Americans do not agree about who they are. This question of identity is nowhere better articulated than in a recent article in the *New York Times* which sought to capture the elusive identities of New York's Italians:

> They are not a closely knit group in any sense. The two great characteristics of the descendants of the immigrants is the pride — frequently unarticulated — they take in being part of the great Romano-Italian civilization, although many of them know very little about it. But mostly, they share an overriding sense of responsibility as American citizens and in that, they are not Italian.
>
> There is disagreement over the number of people of Italian ancestry in the United States, but the best estimate is between 15 million and 20 million, with perhaps 1.5 million in and around New York City. Most are the descendants of immigrants who arrived penniless and illiterate from southern Italy more than half a century ago.

****

> Who are these people and what have they become?
>
> Perhaps their identity has been more defined by motion pictures and television than by anything that might be considered truly Italian. The cinema has presented them as brown of eye, black of hair and red of temper. So great was the demand for swarthy Italian gangster styles some years ago that

an Irishman named J. Carrol Naish made a fortune portraying them in Hollywood.

Many Americans retain an extraordinary image of the Italian immigrant and his descendants as cultural aberrations who sing tenor and peddle fish, and who are romantic, oily, prudish, devious, faithful, sexy, clannish, open-minded, tolerant, intolerant, brilliant, anti-intellectual, unambitious and industrious—all at the same time.

In New York, Italians are stereotyped as garbage collectors who adorn their lawns with plastic flamingos and who sit behind aluminum storm windows in Queens and talk of how Negroes and Puerto Ricans must wait until they are qualified before they get good jobs. The image of the barber who keeps the Madonna on his dashboard remains alive and well.

These impressions have not been altered by the fact that anticlericalism is an older tradition among the Italians than dashboard Madonnas, or by the fact that a survey on race relations conducted recently for the Urban League suggests that Americans other than Italians are far more reactionary.

Whatever his image, the Italian from his very beginnings in America prided himself on how rapidly he was assimilated. Some immigrant parents refused to speak Italian in front of the children so that they could become American that much faster.

****

But on June 29, a remarkable thing happened to the people who have been described as being more American than the Americans. About 40,000 of them, according to the police estimate, gathered at Columbus Circle and waved the Italian tricolor. Perhaps the only Italian word many of them knew was "ciao," but they wore red, white and green buttons calling for "Italian power." After melting in the melting pot for all these years, they looked like they wanted to climb out.

Here was a group New York had taken for granted. But it was also a group that never really considered itself a group, for the Italians and their descendants are notoriously independent of one another. Even in the early days, when they worked for nickels and dimes and were called wops by the immigrants who had gotten there before them, their self-help societies had been weak.

But here they were, reflecting the American proclivity for group defensiveness, joining blacks, Puerto Ricans, Jews, Arabs, Mexicans, Indians, welfare recipients, the aged, conservatives, women, policemen, the New Left, drug advocates, homosexuals and Yippies in protesting for their rights.

If the speech-making at Columbus Circle was taken at face value, those who attended came because they felt that use of the word "Mafia" had smeared and made them suspect. And there is no question that many Italians, even those who did not go to the Unity Day rally, are upset by the use of the word.

****

Why, Italians wonder, is it no longer permissible in respectable circles to use pejoratives to refer to Negroes, Puerto Ricans and Jews, but almost fashionable to direct the same vulgarity at

Italians, and expect them to laugh at "wop," "guinea," "dago" and other terms.[5]

****

How is the neglect of Italian-American past to be explained? The answer is complex, but a number of facts help explain the neglect. The majority of Italians who migrated to the United States during the period of the great migrations (1880-1920) were Southern Italian *contadini,* wretchedly poor and easy marks for manipulative oppression, discrimination and cultural assault:[6] their tardy arrival in America made success and achievement elusive, and more difficult than it had been for earlier peoples (*e.g.,* the Irish); their American-born children were caught in the maelstrom of adaptation (and were clinically studied by a varied cadre of psychologists, social workers, educators and sociologists);[7] in a complex constellation of forces, Italians were the victims of a village-mindedness or provincialism *(Campanilismo)*[8] which they had transplanted from their southern villages of Italy to the teeming ghettos of urban America; and Italians, mystically medieval Catholics, were inhospitably rejected for the

[5]*New York Times,* November 9, 1970.

[6]For a record of the discrimination, see Salvatore J. LaGumina, ed., *Wop: A Documentary History of Anti-Italian Discrimination in the United States* (San Francisco: Straight Arrow Books, 1973).

[7]In 1924, the New York Association for Improving the Condition of the Poor issued a monograph on *The Growth and Development of Italian Children in New York City* which reported on the physical condition of Italian children (*i.e.,* stature; weight; dentition; seasonal variation in growth) with the clinical objectivity and thoroughness of a veterinarian atlas. See John Gebhart (*Entry* no. 228); see also, Irvin L. Child (*Entry* no. 192); Phyllis H. Williams (*Entry* no. 241); and Joseph W. Tait (*Entry* no. 258).

[8]For *campanilismo,* see Leonard Covello (*Entry* no. 253). The word *campanilismo* derives from the words *compana* (bell) and *campanile* (church tower) and "refers to a view of the world that includes reluctance to extend social, cultural, and economic contacts beyond points from which the parish or village bell could be heard." (Joseph Lopreato, *Italian-Americans,* p. 104).

most part by the American Irish Catholic church.[9] Certainly, such a past was not to be envied or nostalgically pursued. And this oppressive burden of the past has been further exacerbated by the stigma of crime: as Alexander DeConde has noted: "In the popular mind, the connecting of Italians with crime was as American as associating Jews with shady business deals, Irishmen with boss politics, or Negroes with watermelons."[10]

The journalist Erik Amfitheatrof (born in Milan of a Russian father and Italian mother, and resident in the United States since age seven) has dealt with this complex cultural phenomenology and (with the liberties allowed journalists) has transmuted it into a felicitously invigorating statement of a still evolving emerging esteem for Italian-Americans:

> Clearly, many Italian-Americans are today responding to the complicated forces loosed by their assimilation into the American mainstream. The children of the Italian immigrants no longer feel Italian. They are American. In shedding a sense of apartness from American life, they have also relinquished their once-powerful emotional associations with a remote Italian world that they knew secondhand, from family recollections and legends. A void has been created, and they are now beginning to reevaluate their ethnic past—which is Italian-American rather than Italian—because it is an inescapable part of what they think about themselves, and what they tell their children. This back-

[9]The best introduction to the evolving relationships of Italian peasants and the American Catholic church is Rudolph J. Vecoli, "Prelates and Peasants: Italian Immigrants and the Catholic Church," *Journal of Social History*, vol. 2 (Spring 1969), pp. 217-268. See also, for a different view, Silvano M. Tomasi's important dissertation (*Entry* no. 279).

[10]Alexander DeConde, *Half Bitter, Half Sweet: An Excursion into Italian American History* (New York: Charles Scribner's Sons, 1971), p. 342.

ward look has been obscured by the issue of the Mafia, which is a great emotional obstruction. When viewed against the background of Italian history, however, the Mafia falls into perspective. It has been overemphasized and overdramatized in the last ten years, and it is, above all, only one aspect of a profound social drama. Far more important than the Mafia to Italian-Americans, as they evaluate their past, is that they can discover a tradition of idealism, and moral and intellectual courage. Yes, the major figures of Italian-American history were great men, but they were great men precisely because they were fighters against their time. They were remarkable individualists, even when their character was flawed, as in the case of Mazzei and Cesnola. The Italian radicals, personified by Ettor and Giovannitti and Carlo Tresca, had uncommon integrity and political courage, and even humble laborers like Sacco and Vanzetti were eloquent in their fidelity to convictions deeply held. The Italians who reached the New World, starting with Columbus, were usually outsiders struggling against great odds, and the best of them were brave, beautiful human beings full of warmth and a large-hearted concern for humanity.[11]

The past, of course, cannot be denied; and the new ethnic consciousness has ushered into being a renaissance of interest in and the study of the Italian-American experience: in recent years, the academic community has witnessed a proliferating number of works which attest to this interest and study, and which suggest an impatience in clearing away the neglect of past decades; and it is hardly fortuitous that

---

[11]Erik Amfitheatrof, *The Children of Columbus: An Informal History of the Italians in the New World* (Boston: Little, Brown, 1973), p. 324.

Italian-American academicians (until the 1960s in little evidence in the colleges and universities) have discovered a cultural *ethos* which relates them to both an enviable minority status and to the new American egalitarianism, and that they have begun exploring the vast, unchartered expanses of their American experiences.

The literature and archives of the Italian-American past assume clearly distinguishable forms. There is, first, a vast literature on Italian emigration to the New World; beyond the statistical records, but clearly part of them, is a corpus of materials which chronicle the migrations, a loosely defined *genre* of voyage-literature, recollections and reminiscences, polemics in behalf of and opposed to the migration (and spilling over into the abrasive literature of native racist restrictionism), and related miscellanea. [12]   In and outside the urban ghettos, a large literature in Italian (for the most part neglected) was generated which responded to the Italian experience in the United States: written by literate Italian immigrants of every persuasion (political pamphleteers and ideologues, journalists, chroniclers, etc.), it awaits translation and source books which will make it available. This is an improvised and tendentious literature which appears under a rich mosaic of imprints, and it is the very substance of the recorded life of the Italian subcommunity, invaluable to the new American historiography.[13] The Italian community was not spared the ministrations of a well-intentioned middle class, and American society was inundated by a flood of tracts, texts, and settlement house materials which sought to solve the "Italian problem:" alternatively condescending and solicitous, this literature is both banal and redemptive, and to which Gino C. Speranza's plaintive "How it Feels to be a

---

[12]For a commentary on the literature of Italian emigration, extant sources and archives, see Silvano M. Tomasi, *The Italians in America* (Occasional Paper. New York: Istituto Italiano di Cultura, 1971).

[13]See Alfredo Bosi and *varia* (*Entry* no. 39); many of these titles are listed in F. Cordasco (*Entry* no. 4).

Problem" is a haughty response.[14] Early scholarly studies
(almost invariably written by non-Italians) extend from Robert F. Foerster's classic, if unimpassioned and icily objective, *The Italian Emigration of Our Time* (1919)[15] to Phyllis
H. Williams' *South Italian Folkways* (1938) and Irvin L.
Child's *Italian or American?* (1943): both of these represent-
ing "late" studies of the intractable Italian minority done
under the auspices of the Yale University Institute of Human
Relations. There is available, too, a not unrespectable corpus
of literary materials produced in the last fifty years by a
competent group of Italian-American novelists and poets, but
this literature has only in the last decade been given any
attention.[16] Beyond a handfull of important early university
dissertations, the serious study of the Italian-American exper-

[14]Gino C. Speranza, "How it Feels to be a Problem: A Consideration of
Certain Causes which Prevent or Retard Assimilation," *Charities*, vol. 20 (April
1908), pp. 55-57. For the settlement house movement, see Allen F. Davis, *Spear-
heads for Reform: The Social Settlements and the Progressive Movement,
1890-1914* (New York: Oxford University Press, 1967); and Allen F. Davis,
American Heroine: The Life and Legend of Jane Addams (New York: Oxford
University Press, 1973).

[15]Robert F. Foerster, *The Italian Emigration of Our Time* (*Entry* no. 26).
"In the specifically Italian districts are many shops providing a single class of
wares, such as Italians are likely to seek. Nothing sells so well as food. A sufficiently modest shop is styled, in Italo-English, a *'grande grosseria italiana.'* Here a
window displays voluminous round cheeses, or strings of sausages, or tinned eels;
round loaves with holes in the center like gigantic doughnuts. Confetti or
macaroni tempts one in another window. Dealers in alcoholic and soft drinks are
many. Here, in combination, are a *'caffé e pasticceria,'* there a bank sells coal.
Some shops become so diversified as to approach the 'general merchandise'
stores of our rural districts. Capitalizing the timidity which the Italian often shows
about trusting many people with his affairs, a very versatile fellow will be at once
a barber, banker, undertaker, wholesale and retail dealer, perhaps also a real estate
and employment agent — yet even such a grotesque association of activities can
hardly be incomprehensible to American patrons of tourists' agencies abroad." (p.
339)

[16]See Rose B. Green (*Entry* no. 154). Wayne Miller (*Entry* no. 166) suggests a reason for the neglect of this literature: "Perhaps one reason for the
neglect is that much of the fiction and poetry that comes out of their minority
experience is critical of the immigrant situation and of the culture at large. Italian-Americans, almost instinctively ignored this literature. What they do not seem
to realize is that their writers, in their very criticism, form a pattern for the
subculture that parallels the pattern for the culture at large." (Miller, p. 27).

ience has been registered in the last few years, and it is this scholarly corpus, together with some retrospective under-pinning and dimensional structure, which my bibliography assembles.

Since my earlier bibliography [17] was retrospective, skele-tal and largely unannotated, I have in the present work con-centrated on recent materials (which are appearing with re-markable rapidity); I have introduced, in most cases, exten-sive annotations, and I have used many of the entries as omnibus bibliographies which permitted a retrospective and dimensional structure: in this sense the present bibliography is both an extension of the earlier bibliography and, in its own right, a new work.

The publication of the present bibliography has also afforded the opportunity to make available invaluable publi-cations of the short-lived Casa Italiana Educational Bureau which had a brief history at Columbia University. I have gathered together Leonard Covello's important statement on the purpose and projected program of the Casa Italiana Edu-cational Bureau; his significant conceptual paradigm on *The Italians in America*; the demographic study of the Italian population in New York by William B. Shedd; and the study of occupational trends of Italians in New York City by John J. D'Alesandre. Together they furnish a rich base of source material for the continuing study of the Italian-American ex-perience.[18]

Of course, the bibliography is not complete: no bibliog-raphy of critical materials can ever hope to be; but it is,

---

[17] F. Cordasco (*Entry* no. 4).

[18] Although the Casa Italiana at Columbia University was built with money raised in the Italian community it was never hospitable to the study of the Italian-American experience; instead, its resources were given over to the study of philology, language instruction and peninsular history. The reason for this hostili-ty to Italian-American life probably is explained in the control of the *Casa Ital-iana* by erstwhile expatriate Northern Italians (*e.g.*, Giuseppe Prezzolini) who were not really part of the Italian-American community. Under Leonard Covello's direction, the Casa Italiana Educational Bureau published in the 1930s the follow-

hopefully, as complete as proved practicable, with the neglect of no important material. I have adopted a flexible structure, facilitating the incorporation of entries: Part I: Bibliography and Archives; Part II: Italian Emigration to America; Part III: Italian American History and Regional Studies (in which I have included notices of Canadian materials, largely on Toronto and its environs); Part IV: Sociology of Italian American Life; Part V: The Political and Economic Context. The frontispiece (from the *Covello Papers, Entry* no. 6) is a street scene in the New York City West Village Italian Community of the early 1920s.

As a sociologist, most of my professional life has been spent among the contemporary poor, in their communities and their institutions (particularly, the schools); this bibliography (and its earlier companion) have taken me back to the antecedents of contemporary poverty, to the grim encounters with continuing patterns of conflict and acculturation, and to the wellsprings of alienation, itself perhaps inevitable in a society as diverse as ours. But the bibliographies have been worthwhile labors (beyond whatever service they afford academicians); they have taken me back to the vanished communities of my youth, and they have added some measure of definition to both my experience and that of my countrymen.

I am indebted to my son, Michael V. Cordasco whose aid makes him a co-author; to my colleague, Dr. Eugene Bucchioni, of City University of New York; to Lydio F. Tomasi and Silvano M. Tomasi of the Center for Migration

---

ing *Bulletins:* (1) *The 11th Annual Report, 1931-1932, Italian Teachers Association;* (2) Peter M. Riccio, *Why English Speaking People Should Study Italian;* (3) Rachel Davis-DuBois, ed., *Some of the Contributions of Italy and Her Sons to Civilization and American Life;* (4) Leonard Covello, *The Casa Italiana Educational Bureau — Its Purpose and Program;* (5) Henry G. Doyle, *The Importance of the Study of the Italian Language;* (6) Leonard Covello, *The Italians in America: With Maps and Research Outlines;* (7) William B. Shedd, *The Italian Population in New York City:* (8) John J. D'Alesandre, *Occupational Trends of Italians in New York City.*

Studies; to my benefactor and mentor, Leonard Covello who, more than anyone else understood the need for the study of the Italian-American experience; and to Angela Barone Jack who, for this project, proved again to be a tireless assistant.

FRANCESCO CORDASCO
January 1974
West New York, New Jersey

I. BIBLIOGRAPHIES
AND
ARCHIVES

I. BIBLIOGRAPHIES AND ARCHIVES

1. THE BALCH INSTITUTE [Philadelphia, Pennsylvania].

An educational institution devoted to North American immigration, ethnic, racial and minority group history. The Institute plans (1974) the construction of a four-story museum and library at Seventh and Ranstead Streets in Philadelphia. The Institute's seven-point program includes: (1) Library programs; (2) Exhibitions; (3) Educational programs; (4) Outreach program; (5) Internal research; (6) Information coordination; (7) Bicentennial planning. The Institute plans to assemble the nation's most comprehensive collection of books, manuscripts and printed materials concerning all national groups who came to North America. Plans call for a library of 400,000 volumes; 20 million manuscripts; 20,000 reels of microfilm; and large numbers of ethnic and minority group newspapers. In November, 1973, the Institute was cataloguing its first 40,000 books. The Balch Institute is supported by trusts established by the late Mrs. Emily Swift Balch and her two sons, Edwin Swift Balch and Thomas Willing Balch.

2. CENTER FOR MIGRATION STUDIES. Brooklyn College, City University of New York.

Organized to "assist scholars in the social sciences, education, humanities, and related fields in the collection, preservation and analysis of primary and secondary materials for the study of the migration processes." An Archives of Migration "will solicit manu-

1

scripts, photographs and taped autobiographies and interviews with significant persons involved in various aspects of migration."

3. CENTER FOR MIGRATION STUDIES [Staten Island, New York].

Address: 209 Flagg Place, Staten Island, New York, 10304. Publishes *The International Migration Review*, a scientific journal studying sociological, demographic, historical, and legislative aspects of migration. Is in process of assembling a specialized library on migration; and a card catalogue of books, articles, and dissertations on migration. Particularly strong (at the present time, the most comprehensive) in its collection of Italian ethnic materials. Maintains connections with Centro Studi Emigrazione (Via della Scrofa 70, Roma 220, Italia), a center staffed by the Society of St. Charles, a religious order ministering to migrants since 1887, which publishes *Studi Emigrazione*.

4. CORDASCO, FRANCESCO. *Italians in the United States: A Bibliography of Reports, Texts, Critical Studies and Related Materials*. New York: Oriole Editions, 1972.

A largely retrospective and unannotated compilation: "The bibliography is not intended to be comprehensive; perhaps, a comprehensive listing is impracticable. Within the framework in which I have structured the entries, I have gathered together a sufficiently representative literature to afford both orientation and resources for further study." Includes a "Preliminary Checklist of Novels Written in English Dealing with the Italian American Experience."

5. CORDASCO, FRANCESCO. "The Children of Columbus: Recent Works on the Italian-American Experience," *Phylon: The Atlanta University Review of Race and Culture*, vol. 4 (September 1973), pp. 295-298.

6. COVELLO PAPERS [East Harlem, New York City Italian Community].

   A rich collection of reports, papers, correspondence and memorabilia collected by Leonard Covello (1887-   ) on the life of the largest Italian community in the United States. [c. 1915-1945] In possession of F. Cordasco.

7. DORE, GRAZIA. *La Democrazia e l'Emigrazione in America.* Brescia: Morcelliana, 1964.

   Includes "Bibliografia Per la Storia Dell'Emigrazione Italiana in America," pp. 381-493. "Le ricerche da noi fatte si limitano a quel periodo dell'emigrazione transoceanica che va dal suo inizio agli anni verso il 1927, a quando, cioè, con la soppressione del Commisseriato, si chiudeva, anche formalmente, una fase del fenomeno emigratorio."

8. FIRKENS, INA TEN EYCK. "Italians in the United States," *Bulletin of Bibliography*, vol. 8 (January 1915), pp. 129-133.

9. HOWERTON, JOSEPH B. "The Resources of the National Archives For Ethnic Research," *The Immigration History Newsletter*, vol. 5 (November 1973), pp. 1-8.

   Adapted from a paper read at the Chicago Regional Archives—De Paul University Symposium on Ethnic Research (Chicago: De Paul University, April 28, 1973).

10. IL BOLLETINO DELL'EMIGRAZIONE [1903-   ].

Published by the Italian Ministry. An invaluable source of information on Italian settlements. See, *e.g.,* G.E. Di Palma Di Castiglione, "Dove possono andare gli Italiani Immigranti negli Stati Uniti," *Boll. dell'Emigrazione* (1909); "Intorno a un Nuovo Progetto sulla Immigrazione negli Stati Uniti," *Boll. dell'Emigrazione* (1924); "Legislazione sull'Emigrazione e sull'Emigrazione negli Stati Uniti," *Boll. dell'Emigrazione* (1906); A. Panerazi, "Condizione di Lavoro e politica immigratoria negli Stati Uniti," *Boll. dell'Emigrazione* (1919); "Statistica dell'Emigrazione Italiana," *Boll. dell'Emigrazione* (1902-1925, *passim*).

11. THE INTERNATIONAL MIGRATION REVIEW. Vol. I (New Series), 1965-

Includes bibliographical notes; reviews of books; and an invaluable "Review of Reviews," abstracts of important publications in migration literature. See also, *The Immigration History Newsletter* (Minnesota Historical Society, 1971-   ); and *Ethnicity: An Interdisciplinary Journal of the Study of Ethnic Relations* (Academic Press, 1974-   ).

12. ITALIAN BIBLIOGRAPHY. New York: Service Bureau for Intercultural Education, 1936.

13. [ITALIANS]. New York Public Library. *[The] Italian People in the United States.* New York: The Library, 1936. 2 vols.

A collection of clippings and pamphlets.

14. [ITALIANS]. "A Selected List of Bibliographical References and Records of the Italians in the United States," *Italian Library of Information.* Outline Series; Series 1, No. 5 (August 1958), pp. 1-19.

15. TOMASI, SILVANO M. *The Italians in America.* Occasional Paper. New York: Istituto Italiano di Cultura, July 1971.

    Largely a bibliographical essay on sources for the study of Italian emigration, and the Italian experience in America.

16. THE UNIVERSITY OF MINNESOTA, IMMIGRANT ARCHIVES.

    Address: Immigrant Archives, University Library, University of Minnesota, Minneapolis, Minnesota, 55455. An international center for the collection and preservation of the historical records of immigrants who came to the United States and Canada from Eastern and Southern Europe. See Rudolph J. Vecoli, "The Immigration Studies Collection of the University of Minnesota," *American Archivist,* vol. 32 (April 1969), pp. 139-145.

17. VECOLI, RUDOLPH J. "The Immigration Studies Collection of the University of Minnesota," *American Archivist,* vol. 32 (April 1969), pp. 139-145.

    Includes Italian materials.

18. VELIKONJA, JOSEPH. *Italians in the United States.* Occasional Papers, No. 1. Department of Geography, Southern Illinois University, Carbondale, Illinois: 1963.

A pioneer compilation and unannotated list on the Italian experience in the United States. Some copies of the mimeographed list are miscollated. See review, with corrections, Joseph G. Fucilla, *Italica,* vol. 41 (June 1964), pp. 213-216.

II. ITALIAN EMIGRATION TO AMERICA

II. ITALIAN EMIGRATION TO AMERICA

19. BRENNA, PAOLO G. *Storia dell'Emigrazione Italiana.* Roma: Libreria Cremonese, 1928.

   See also, Luigi Villari, *Gli Stati Uniti d'America e l'Emigrazione Italiana* (Milano: Fratelli Treves, 1912); and G.E. Di Palma Di Castiglione, *L'Immigrazione Italiana negli Stati Uniti d'America dal 1820 al 30 Giugno 1910* (Roma: Tip. Cartiere Centrali, 1913); and Brenna's earlier *L'emigrazione Italiana nel periodo ante bellico* (Firenze, 1918).

20. CAVANAUGH, FRANCES P. *Immigration Restriction at Work Today: A Study of the Administration of Immigration Restriction by the United States.* Catholic University of America, 1928. (unpublished doctoral dissertation).

   See also, John Higham, *Stranger in the Land: Patterns of American Nativism, 1860-1925* (New York: Atheneum, 1963); and Thomas F. Gossett, *Race: The History of an Idea in America* (Dallas: Southern Methodist University Press, 1963) which deals with nativism, immigration and restriction, and with reference to Italians. For the backgrounds of anti-foreignism and restrictionism, see John Higham, "Origins of Immigration Restriction, 1882-1897: A Social Analysis." *Mississippi Valley Historical Review,* vol. 39 (June 1952), pp. 77-88.

21. CIUCCI, L. "Stima Delle Migrazioni Nette per Generazioni in Italia nel periodo 1951-1961," *Genus,* vol. 27 (1971), pp. 29-58.

22. DELLA PERUTA, FRANCO. "Per la Storia dell'Emigrazione Meridionale," *Nuova Revista Storica*, Nos. 3-4 (1965), pp. 344-356.

A review of the literature on Italian emigration and emigration in the 1950's and 1960's. See also, "The Italian Experience in Emigration," *International Migration Review*, ed. by S.M. Tomasi, vol. I (Summer 1967) which includes a wide range of articles.

23. DICKINSON, ROBERT E. *The Population Problem of Southern Italy*. Syracuse: Syracuse University Press, 1955, (unpublished doctoral dissertation)

See also, A. Rodgers, "Migration and Industrial Development: The Southern Italian Experience," *Southern Geography*, vol. 46 (April 1970), pp. 111-135.

24. DIVINE, ROBERT A. *American Immigration Policy, 1924-1952*. New Haven: Yale University Press, 1957.

Restriction and its aftermath.

25. DORE, GRAZIA. "Some Social and Historical Aspects of Italian Emigration to America," *Journal of Social History* (Winter 1968), pp. 95-122.

An examination of the social and historical environment from which the emigration developed. Reprinted in F. Cordasco, *The Italians: Social Backgrounds of an American Group* (1974).

26. FOERSTER, ROBERT F. *The Italian Emigration of Our Times*. Cambridge: Harvard University Press, 1919.

Reissued with an introductory note by F. Cordasco, New York : Russell & Russell, 1968.

A classic study of the mass Italian migrations to all parts of the world between 1880-1919. Vast bibliographical footnotes affording the best guide to the literature of Italian emigration. See also, Antonio Stella, *Some Aspects of Italian Immigration to the United States: Statistical Data Based Chiefly Upon the U.S. Census and Other Official Publications* (New York: G.P. Putnam's Sons, 1924: Reprinted, San Francisco: R & E Research Associates, 1970). See also, R. Paolucci De Calboli, *Larmes et Sourires de l'Emigration Italienne* (Paris, 1909); and Foerster's "A Statistical Survey of Italian Emigration," *Quarterly Journal of Economics,* vol. 23 (November 1909), pp. 66-103. A valuable overview of reactions to Italian migration is in Salvatore Mondello, "Italian Migration to the United States as reported in American Magazines, 1880-1920," *Social Science,* vol. 39 (June 1964), pp. 131-142.

27. FONTANI, ALVO. *Gli Emigrati: L'Altra Faccia del "Miracolo Economico."* Roma, 1962.

28. GANS, HERBERT J. "Some Comments on the History of Italian Migration and on the Nature of Historical Research," *International Migration Review,* vol. I (Summer 1967), pp. 5-9.

29. GILKEY, GEORGE R. "The United States and Italy: Migration and Repatriation," *Journal of Developing Areas* (1967), pp. 23-35.

See also, Francesco Cervase, "L'Emigrazione di Retorno nel Processo di Integrazione dell'Immigrato: Una Prima Formulazione," *Genus,* vol. 23 (1967); and the major study by Antonio Perotti, *Programmazione e Rientro degli Emigranti* (Roma: Centro Studi Emigrazione, 1967). A Valuable historical overview of repatriation is Betty B. Caroli, *Italian Repatriation From The United States, 1900-1914* (Staten Island: Center For Migration Studies, 1973); reference should also be made to Francesco Bolletta, *Il Banco di Napoli e le Rimesse degli Emigrati* (Napoli: Istituto Internazionale, 1972).

30. HANDLIN, OSCAR. *A Pictorial History of Immigration.* New York: Crown Publishers, 1972.

See also, Ann Novotny, *Strangers at the Door: Ellis Island, Castle Garden, and the Great Migration to America* (Riverside, Conn.: Chatham Press, 1971); Allon Schoener, ed., *Portal to America: The Lower East Side, 1870-1925* (New York: Holt, Rinehart, Winston, 1967); and for an Italian view of Ellis Island, see Ludovico Caminata, *Nell'Isola delle Lagrime: Ellis Island* (New York: Stabilimento Tipografico Italia, 1924). See also, Edward Corsi, *In the Shadow of Liberty: The Chronicle of Ellis Island* (New York: Macmillan, 1937).

31. HIGHAM, JOHN. "From Immigrants to Minorities: Some Recent Literature," *American Quarterly,* vol. 10 (Spring 1958), pp. 83-88.

32. LIVI-BACCI, MASSIMO. *L'Immigrazione e l'Assimilazione degli Italiani negli Stati Uniti Secondo le Statistiche demografiche Americane.* Milano: Giuffrè, 1961.

Estimates that there were in 1950 in the United States no fewer than seven million people, belonging to three generations, who had at least one Italian grandparent. Other estimates have run as high as twenty-one million and over. See Giuseppe Lucrezio Monticelli, "Italian Emigration: Basic Characteristics and Trends," in S.M. Tomasi and M.H. Engels, eds., *The Italian Experience in the United States* (1970), pp. 3-22; and Joseph Velikonja, "The Italian born in the United States, 1950," Annals of the *Association of American Geographers,* vol. 51 (December 1961).

33. LOPREATO, JOSEPH. *Effects of Emigration on the Social Structure of a Calabrian Community.* Yale University, 1960. (unpublished doctoral dissertation)

See the author's *Peasants No More: Social Class and Social Change in an Underdeveloped Society* (San Francisco: Chandler Publishing Co., 1967); and Manlio A. D'Ambrosio, *Il Mezzogiorno d'Italia e l'Emigrazione negli Stati Uniti* (Roma: Athenaeum, 1924). For Southern Italian society, see Edward C. Banfield, *The Moral Basis of a Backward Society* (New York: Free Press, 1958); and Carlo Levi, *Christ Stopped at Eboli,* trans. by Frances Frenaye (New York: Farrar, Straus, and Giroux, 1969). For emigration out of the South, see Giovanni Bonacci, *Calabria e Emigrazione* (Firenze: Ricci, 1908).

34. LUCREZIO, M.G., and L. FAVERO. "Un Quarto di Secolo di Emigrazione Italiana," *Studi Emigrazione,* vol. 9 (May-June 1972), pp. 25-26; 5-91.

Italian emigration during the last twenty-five years and its prospects for coming years. See also, M. Federici, *Emigrazione Ieri e Domani* (Roma: Edizione Associazione Nazionale Famiglia degli Emigrati, 1972).

35. PITKIN, DONALD S. *Land Tenure and Family Organization in an Italian Village.* Harvard University, 1954. (unpublished doctoral dissertation)

On the relationship between the nuclear and extended family in Italian culture, see Constance Cronin, *The Sting of Change* (Chicago: University of Chicago Press, 1970); see also, Aubrey Menen, "The Italian Family is a Commune," *New York Times Magazine,* March 1, 1970; and Sydel F. Silverman, "An Ethnographic Approach to Social Stratification: Prestige in a Central Italian Community," *American Anthropologist,* vol. 68 (August 1966), pp. 899-922.

36. SCHACHTER, J. "Net Immigration of Gainful Workers into the United States, 1870-1930." *Demography,* vol. 9 (February 1972), pp. 87-105.

37. TOMASI, S.M. "Italian Immigration to the United States," *Migration News,* vol. 19 (1970), pp. 3-8.

Contemporary immigration from Italy with an analysis of immigration to the United States for its quantitative aspects, and the economic and religious backgrounds of southern Italian immigrants.

III. ITALIAN AMERICAN
HISTORY AND REGIONAL STUDIES

III. ITALIAN-AMERICAN HISTORY
AND REGIONAL STUDIES

A. *GENERAL STUDIES & RELATED MATERIALS*

38. AMFITHEATROF, ERIK. *The Children of Columbus: An Informal History of the Italians in the New World.* Boston: Little, Brown, 1973.

A series of vignette-like chapters held together loosely in an historical framework. Includes Italian backgrounds ("The Navigators"; "The Fall of the Renaissance"; "Risorgimento," etc.) followed by impressionistic tableaux, each assigned a chapter, *e.g.*, the South; Mulberry Bend; Little Italies; the Turbulent Thirties, etc. See review, Andrew Rolle, *International Migration Review,* vol. 7 (Winter 1973), pp. 478-479.

39. BOSI, ALFREDO. *Cinquanti'anni di Vita Italiana in America.* New York: Bagnasco Press, 1921.

Part of a large (essentially neglected) literature on the Italian communities in America in the form of narratives, reminiscences, etc. See, *e.g.*, Amy Bernardi, *America Vissuta* (Torino: Fratelli Bocca Editori, 1911); Filidelfio Caruso, *Ricordo dei Benemeriti Italiani d'America* (New York: Caruso, 1908); Gaetano Conte, *Dieci Anni in America: Impressioni e Ricordi* (Palermo: G. Spinnato, 1903); Giuseppe Giacosa, *Impressioni d'America* (Milano: T.F. Cogliati, 1908); Adolfo Rossi, *Nel Paese dei Dollari: Tre Anni a New York* (Milano: Kantorvinz, 1893); Leone S. Arrigioni, *Un Viaggio in America: Impressioni* (Torino: Tipografia Salesiana, 1906); Gaspare Nicotri, *Dalla Conca d'Oro al "Golden Gate": Studi e Impressioni di Viaggio in America* (New York: Canorna Press, 1928).

40. CAPPONI, GUIDO. *Italy and Italian in Early American Periodicals, 1741-1830.* University of Wisconsin, 1958. (unpublished doctoral dissertation)

41. COLAJANNI, NAPOLEONE. *Gli Italiani negli Stati Uniti.* Roma-Napoli: Presso La Rivista Popolare, 1910.

42. CORDASCO, FRANCESCO. *Jacob Riis Revisited: Poverty and the Slum in Another Area.* New York: Doubleday, 1968.

    Selections from Jacob Riis's *How the Other Half Lives* (1890); *The Children of the Poor* (1892); and *A Ten Years' War* (1900), all of which contain material on immigrant Italians in New York City. See also, Riis's "Feast Days in Little Italy," *The Century Magazine,* vol. 58 (August 1899), pp. 491-499.

43. CORDASCO, FRANCESCO and EUGENE, BUCCHIONI. *The Italians: Social Backgrounds of an American Group.* Clifton, N.J.: Augustus M. Kelley, 1974.

    A documentary sourcebook on the Italians in the United States, largely between 1880 and 1940. Includes: (I) Emigration: The Exodus of a Latin People; (II) Italian Communities in America: Campanilismo in the Ghetto; (III) Responses to American Life; (IV) Employment, Health and Social Needs; (V) Education: The Italian Child in the American School; Bibliography. Includes 16 halftone reproductions and frontispiece.

44. DeCONDE, ALEXANDER. *Half Bitter, Half Sweet: An Excursion into Italian American History.* New York: Charles Scribner's Sons, 1971.

Political highlights of the Italo-American relationship, economic ties, cultural interplay, and the effects produced in both countries by the massive emigration of Italians to the United States. Includes an extensive bibliography.

45. DOUGLAS, DAVID W. *Influence of the Southern Italian in American Society.* New York: Columbia University, 1915. (Columbia University Studies in Sociology)

46. ETS, MARIE HALL. *Rosa: The Life of an Italian Immigrant.* Foreword by Rudolph J. Vecoli. Minneapolis: University of Minnesota Press, 1970.

Narrative by a social worker at the Chicago Commons (World War I and after) of life of Italian immigrant peasant woman, assembled out of stories told by Rosa of her early life and experiences.

47. IORIZZO, LUCIANO J., and SALVATORE MONDELLO. *The Italian-Americans.* New York: Twayne Publishers, 1971.

"We have attempted to present the Italian immigration as an integral part of American history rather than as an isolated social phenomenon." Selects the Italians of Oswego, New York, as examples of the experiences of "the newcomers in small-town America."

48. [ISTITUTO DI STUDI AMERICANI] *Gli Italiani negli Stati Uniti.* Università degli Studi di Firenze, 1972.

Proceedings of the Third Symposium of American Studies, organized by the University of Florence on

May 27-29, 1969. The 21 papers presented deal with various aspects of Italian emigration into North America: R.J. Vecoli, "American Sources for the Study of the Italian Immigration"; G. Barbieri, "For a Draft of Researches of Emigration in America"; L. Bertelli, "Elite and Mass Culture in the Italian Emigration to the U.S."; M. Ciacci, "Notes of the Linguistic Behavior of Italian Emigrants in the U.S."; E. Del Vecchio, "The Italian Emigration to the U.S. as a Means of Enriching the Development of Commercial Relations"; L. J. Iorizzo, "A Re-evaluation of the Leadership in Italian Immigrant Communities in New York State"; S.J. La Gumina, "Immigrants and Politics—Conservatives and Liberals: The Case of the Italian Americans"; J.S. McDonald, "Structure and Affinity in the Characteristics of the Italian-American Community: Problems of Organization and Social Sponsorship"; A. Marsellone, "The Study of Emigration in American Historiography"; S. Mondello, "Crime, Italian Immigrants, and the Press, 1880-1920"; P. Nazzaro, "The Immigration Quota Act of 1921"; N.P. Corbella, "History of an Italian Worker's Union in New York: the Tailors"; M. Sylvers, "Italian Socialists in Houston, Texas, 1896-98"; S.M. Tomasi, "Americanization or Pluralism? The Ethnic Italian Church as Intermediary Agent in the Process of Integrating the Immigrants in the U.S."; J. Velikonja, "The Italian Contribution to the Geographical Character of Tontitown, Arkansas, and Rosati, Missouri"; T. Tosi, "The Emigration from Barga, Italy, from its Beginnings until the Present"; P. Russo, "The Italo-American Periodical Press."

49. [ITALIANS] *International Migration Review,* vol. I, New Series (Summer 1967).

Entire issue devoted to Italian-American experience, ("Special Issue: The Italian Experience in Emigration"), with considerable bibliography.

50. LA FALCE, ALFONSO. "An Italian in America," *Life,* vol. 35 (October 5, 1953), pp. 134-144.

See discussion, *Ibid.,* October 26, 1953, p. 12. On the Italian family in America.

51. LO GATTO, ANTHONY F. *The Italians in America, 1492-1972.* Dobbs Ferry, N.Y.: Oceana Publications, 1973.

A skeletal chronology, and collection of documents, with a list of prominent Italian-Americans.

52. LOPREATO, JOSEPH. *Italian-Americans.* New York: Random House, 1970.

A brief overview and sociological portrait. "Represents a sociologist's efforts to summarize and, where possible, bring up to date our knowledge of major aspects of the Italian-Americans' social experience as they bear on their continuing assimilation."

53. LORD, ELLIOT, JOHN D. TRENNER, and SAMUEL BARROWS. *The Italian in America.* New York: B.F. Buck and Co., 1906. Reprinted, San Francisco: R & E Research Associates, 1970.

An early influential history. Other early accounts include: Philip M. Rose, *The Italians in America* (New York: George H. Doran, 1922); Francis E. Clark, *Our Italian Fellow Citizens in Their Old Homes and Their New* (Boston: Small, Maynard & Co., 1919); Sarah G.

Pomeroy, *The Italian* (New York: Fleming H. Rovell Co., 1915), a widely circulated bulletin; Antonio Stella, *The Effects of Urban Congestion on Italian Women and Children* (New York: William Wood, 1908), a general account of conditions in New York City.

54. MANGIONE, JERRE. *America Is Also Italian.* New York: G.P. Putnam's Sons, 1969.

One of a series of volumes "telling the important stories of immigrant groups." Intended for young readers. Also intended for young readers is Barbara Marinacci, *They Came from Italy: The Story of Famous Italian Americans* (New York: Dodd, 1967); see also, S. La Gumina, *An Album of the Italian American* (New York: Franklin Watts, 1972); Ronald P. Grossman, *The Italians in America* (Minneapolis: Lerner Publications, 1966); and Anthony Lombardo, *The Italians In America* (Chicago: Claretian Publications, 1973).

55. MONDELLO, SALVATORE A. *The Italian Immigrant in Urban America, 1880-1920, as Reported in the Contemporary Periodical Press.* New York University, 1960. (unpublished doctoral dissertation)

56. MOQUIN, WAYNE, with CHARLES VAN DOREN. *A Documentary History of the Italian Americans.* New York: Praeger, 1974.

Includes (I) Italian American Presence in the New World, 1492-1850; (II) Immigrations and Patterns of Settlement, 1850-1929; (III) Making a Living, 1890-1930; (IV) Quasi-Public Utility: Organized Crime in the Italian American Community; (V) Controversy Over Italian American Immigration: Violence and Polemic; (VI) The Emergence of the Italian Americans.

57. MUSMANNO, MICHAEL A. *The Story of the Italians in America.* New York: Doubleday, 1965.

An uncritical account of the success of Italians in the United States.

58. PISANI, LAWRENCE F. *The Italian in America: A Social Study and History.* New York: Exposition Press, 1957.

A sociological interpretation.

59. ROLLE, ANDREW F. *The American Italians: Their History and Culture.* Belmont, California: Wadsworth Publishing Company, 1972.

"An historical approach to the immigrant experience·. . . describing why immigrants left Italy, how they were changed by American culture, how they fared and where they settled." An historical primer intended to open up "minority studies to young people" and to meet a "social and educational need." See also the author's *The Immigrant Upraised: Italian Adventurers and Colonists in an Expanding America* (Norman: University of Oklahoma Press, 1968), which traces the history of Italian immigrants in the American West in some 22 states west of the Mississippi.

60. SALVADORI, MASSIMO. *A Pictorial History of the Italian People.* New York: Crown Publishers, 1972.

61. SCHIAVO, GIOVANNI E. *Four Centuries of Italian-American History.* New York: The Vigo Press, 1952. Revised edition, 1958.

See also the author's *Italian-American History*, 2 vols. (New York: Vigo Press, 1947-1949); *The Italians in America Before the Civil War* (New York: G.P. Putnam's Sons, 1924; 1934); *The Italians in Chicago: A Study in Americanization* (Chicago: Italian-American Publishing Co., 1928), which includes a preface by Jane Addams; *The Italians in Missouri* (Chicago: Italian-American Publishing Co., 1929). Schiavo also edited *The Italian-American Who's Who* (1935-*irregular*).

62. TOMASI, LYDIO F., ed. *The Italian in America: The Progressive View, 1891-1914.* New York: Center for Migration Studies, 1972.

Brings together out of the progressive journal, *Charities,* a significant corpus of materials (1894-1913) which deal with the Italian immigrant. Materials are on immigration, assimilation, labor abuses, housing and social conditions, crime and criminality, health and the scourge of tuberculosis. Reviewed (with other works), F. Cordasco, *Phylon: The Atlanta Review of Race and Culture,* vol. 4 (September 1973), pp. 295-298. See also, Salvatore Mondello, "The Magazine *Charities* and the Italian Immigrants," *Journalism Quarterly,* vol. 44 (Spring 1967), pp. 91-98.

63. TOMASI, SILVANO M., and MADELINE H. ENGEL, eds. *The Italian Experience in the United States.* New York: Center for Migration Studies, 1970.

Includes materials on Italian emigration; Italian immigrants in the United States; the *Padrone* system; Italians in urban America; Italians and organized labor; the immigrant child; Italo-American politicians; religious acculturation of Italians; return migration to Italy.

B. *REGIONAL STUDIES*

a. *THE NORTHEAST*

64. ANDERSON, NELS. *The Social Antecedents of a Slum: A Developmental Study of the East Harlem Area of Manhattan Island, New York City.* New York University, 1930. (unpublished doctoral dissertation)

    The East Harlem (New York City) Italian community.

65. BIANCO, CARLA. *The Two Rosetos.* Bloomington: Indiana University Press, 1974.

    Study of an Italian-American community in Pennsylvania where the inhabitants have kept nearly intact much of the culture, folklore, and dialect brought from their "sister" village in southern Italy. See also, Clement L. Valletta, *A Study of Americanization in Carneta: Italian American Identity through Three Generations,* University of Pennsylvania, 1968. (Unpublished doctoral dissertation)

66. CHURCHILL, CHARLES W. *The Italians of Newark: A Community Study.* New York University, 1942. (unpublished doctoral dissertation)

    See also, Grace Irwin, "Michelangelo in Newark," *Harper's Magazine,* vol. 143 (September 1921), pp. 446-454.

67. CIMILLUCA, SALVATORE. *The Natural History of East Harlem from Eighteen Eighty to the Present Day.* New York University, 1931. (unpublished M.A. thesis)

East Harlem, New York City. "The study, which stresses the outstanding forces in the development of East Harlem, constitutes a foundation for a more detailed and extensive study of the history of the area for the same period." Extensive notices of Italian community.

68. CONCISTRE, MARIE J. *Adult Education in a Local Area: A Study of a Decade in the Life and Education of the Adult Immigrant in East Harlem, New York City.* New York University, 1943. (unpublished doctoral dissertation)

The full "round-of-life" of the Italian subcommunity of East Harlem. Provides detailed vignettes of Italian traditions and heritages; the Italian family; language difficulties of immigrant groups; the Italian and politics; economic status and housing; mobility and social effects; and of the multiplicity of Italian religious institutions which flourished.

69. CORDASCO, FRANCESCO, and ROCCO GALAT-TIOTO. "Ethnic Displacement in the Interstitial Community: The East Harlem [New York City] Experience," *Phylon: The Atlanta Review of Race and Culture,* vol. 31 (Fall 1970), pp. 302-312.

The Italian community in East Harlem and its displacement, with notices of Puerto Rican, Black, and Jewish communities.

70. CRESSEY, PAUL C. *The Social Role of the Motion Picture in an Interstitial Area.* New York University, 1942. (unpublished doctoral dissertation)

"Intervals" is a code name for East Harlem, New

York City. Italian teenagers were heavily influenced by motion pictures. Maintains that Italian teenagers who attended movies frequently were not likely to participate in a significant way in organized recreation offered by the settlement houses.

71. DICKINSON, JOAN Y. "Aspects of Italian Immigration to Philadelphia," *Pennsylvania Magazine of History and Biography,* vol. 40 (October 1966), pp. 445-465.

An overview from the colonial era to the present. See also, Sister M. Agnes Gertrude, "Italian Immigration into Philadelphia," *Records of the American Catholic Historical Society,* vol. 58 (1947); and Ernesto L. Biagi, *The Italians of Philadelphia* (1967); for an early account, see Emily W. Dinwiddie, "Some Aspects of Italian Housing and Social Conditions in Philadelphia," *Charities,* vol. 12 (May 1904), pp. 490-494.

72. ERNST, ROBERT. *Immigrant Life in New York City, 1825-1863.* New York: King's Crown Press, 1949.

New York's earliest "Little Italy."

73. FONZI, GAETON J. "Philadelphia's Italians: A Bubbly Minestrone," *Greater Philadelphia Magazine* (January 1961), pp. 24-28; 66-69.

74. GHIRADELLA, ROMEO. *The Social Organization of Work among Italians in New York City.* Columbia University, 1929. (unpublished M.A. thesis)

75. GLAZER, NATHAN, and DANIEL P. MOYNIHAN. *Beyond the Melting Pot: The Negroes, Puerto Ricans, Jews, Italians, and Irish of New York City.* Cambridge: M.I.T. Press, 2nd ed., 1970.

The section on Italians was written by Glazer. Concerns itself with community, family influences, religion, occupations, and politics.

76. JONES, THOMAS J. *Sociology of a New York City Block.* Columbia University, 1908 (Studies in Sociology).

77. JULIANI, RICHARD N. *The Social Organization of Immigration: The Italians in Philadelphia.* University of Pennsylvania, 1971. (unpublished doctoral dissertation)

Examines the social organization of immigration as an alternative to the more usual research on the demographic aspects of international migration or the social psychology of assimilation. Basic data were obtained through a series of tape-recorded oral histories provided by Italian-born male immigrants between 66 and 93 years old who came to the United States between 1894 to 1924. Findings: Italian immigration passed through three major stages in Philadelphia: (1) the "adventurer" stage; (2) the *padroni* stage; (3) and the *paesani* stage. Each stage was distinct in terms of the character of the migrants, their intentions and motives, and the social processes and relations which made it possible.

78. McLAUGHLIN, VIRGINIA Y. *Like the Fingers of the Hand: The Family and Community Life of First Generation Italian-Americans in Buffalo, New York, 1880-1930.* State University of New York at Buffalo, 1970. (unpublished doctoral dissertation)

Demographic data indicates that conservative family

migration patterns contributed to family stability in America. Conservative female occupational arrangements conforming to Italian ethnic traditions prevailed. Analysis of Italian community life, and the unsuccessful efforts of charity and welfare workers with the immigrant poor, indicate the Italians' tendency to organize their family and social affairs along personal and familiar rather than institutional lines. Italo-American family behavior in the United States was partially a product of Italian peasant origins. Buffalo's Italians developed a family life style which can in fact be designated as working class. That family attitudes and behavior were differentiated by class suggests that class, not ethnicity alone, had a significant impact upon the immigrant family. See the author's "Patterns of Work and Family Organization: Buffalo's Italians," *The Journal of Interdisciplinary History,* vol. 2 (Autumn, 1971), pp. 299-314.

79. MANGANO, ANTONIO. *Italian Colonies in New York City.* Columbia University, 1904. (Studies in Sociology)

80. MARIANO, JOHN H. *The Second Generation of Italians in New York City.* New York University, 1921. (Ph.D. dissertation)

   Published as *The Italian Contribution to American Democracy* (Boston: Christopher Publishing House, 1921).

81. MIGLIORE, SALVATORE. *Half a Century of Italian Immigration into Pittsburgh and Allegheny County.* University of Pittsburgh, 1928. (unpublished M.A. thesis)

82. "New York's Italians: A Question of Identity Within and Without." *New York Times,* November 9, 1970.

    See also, Mario Puzo, "The Italians, American Style," *New York Times Magazine,* August 6, 1967; and reactions, *Ibid.,* August 20, 1967; September 10, 1967.

83. SANGRE, WALTER H. *Mel Hyblaeum: A Study of the People of Middletown of Sicilian Extraction.* Wesleyan University, 1952. (unpublished M.A. thesis)

84. SOLOMON, BARBARA M. *Ancestors and Immigrants: A Changing New England Tradition.* Cambridge: Harvard University Press, 1956.

    Italians in New England.

85. TANGARONE, ADAM. *An Intensive Study of the Torrington Italian Mission Connected with the Center Congregational Church, Torrington, Connecticut.* Hartford School of Religious Education, 1935. (unpublished M.R.E. thesis)

86. THERNSTROM, STEPHAN. *The Other Bostonians: Poverty and Progress in the American Metropolis, 1880-1970.* Cambridge: Harvard University Press, 1973.

    Uses the social statistics of the city seeking "the fullest series of observations ever made of patterns of migration and social mobility in a changing American community."

87. TILLEY, MARGARET C. *The Boy Scout Movement in East Harlem.* New York University, 1935. (unpublished doctoral dissertation)

East Harlem, New York City. Concludes that program failed among East Harlem Italian youth because it had no value "as a technique for instilling positive character traits."

88. TOMANIO, ANTHONY J., and LUCILLE N. La MACCHIA. *The Italian-American Community in Bridgeport.* University of Bridgeport, 1953. (Bridgeport Community Area Study. Student Monograph, no. 5).

Studies the social institutions of Italian Americans in Bridgeport, their acculturation to the community, and the extent to which they have preserved elements of their original Italian culture.

89. UNITED STATES FEDERAL WRITERS PROJECT. New York City. *The Italians of New York.* A Survey Prepared by Workers of the Federal Writers Project. Work Progress Administration in the City of New York. New York: Random House, 1938. [Published also in Italian]

90. WARD, DAVID. "The Emergence of Central Immigrant Ghettoes in American Cities, 1840-1920," *Annals of the Association of American Geographers,* vol. 58 (June 1968), pp. 343-359.

Boston's Italian community.

91. WARE, CAROLINE F. *Greenwich Village, 1920-1930. A Comment on American Civilization in the Post-War Years.* New York: Harper, 1935; reissued with a new preface, 1965.

Includes "The Italian Community," pp. 152-202; and A.E. Bromsen, "The Public School's Contribution to the Maladaptation of the Italian Boy," pp. 455-461.

b. *THE SOUTH*

92. [ARKANSAS] "A model Italian Community in Arkansas," *Review of Reviews,* vol. 34 (September 1906), pp. 361-362.

93. AARONSON, R. R. "Pecan Tree," *Common Ground,* vol. 10 (1949), pp. 75-88.

Sicilians in New Orleans.

94. CARACHRIST, C. F. Z. "Italian Immigration to the South," *Manufacturers' Record* (August 1905).

95. CHIESI, GUSTAVO. *La nostra Emigrazione negli Stati Uniti e la Colonizzazione nel Texas.* Roma: Unione Tipografica Cooperativa, 1908.

96. CLARK, ELMER T. *The Latin Immigrant in the South.* Nashville: Cokesbury Press, 1924.

97. HEWES, LESLIE: "Tontitown: Ozark Vineyard Center," *Economic Geography,* vol. 29 (April 1953), pp. 125-143.

The Italian community and how it developed.

98. LANGLEY, LEE J. "The Italian as a Southern Farmer: Striking Characterization of their Success and Value to the Community," *Manufacturers' Record* (August 1904).

See also, the author's "Italians in the Cotton Field: Their Superiority over Negroes Shown on an Arkansas Plantation," *Manufacturers' Record* (April 1904).

99. MEADE, EMILY F. "Italian Immigration into the South," *South Atlantic Quarterly*, vol. 4 (July 1905), pp. 217-223.

See also, Albert Phenis, "Italian Immigration to the South," *Manufacturers' Record* (May 1905).

100. PANOGOPOULOS, E. P. *New Smyrna: An Eighteenth Century Greek Odyssey.* University of Florida, 1966. (unpublished doctoral dissertation)

Data on Italian settlers.

101. RAMIREZ, M. D. "Italian Folklore from Tampa, Florida," *Southern Folklore Quarterly*, vol. 13 (June 1949), pp. 121-132; 101-106.

102. ROSELLI, BRUNO. *The Italians in Colonial Florida: A Repository of Italian Families settled in Florida under Spanish (1513-1762; 1784-1821) and British (1762-1784) Regimes.* Jacksonville: Drew Press, 1940.

103. SCARPACI, JEAN. *Italian Immigrants in Louisiana's Sugar Parishes: Recruitment, Labor Conditions, and Community Relations, 1880-1910.* Rutgers University, 1972. (unpublished doctoral dissertation)

Deals with phenomena of immigration from Sicily to the southern United States, immigrants in agriculture, immigrant-black relations, and the active recruitment efforts of Louisiana to obtain laborers from southern

Europe from 1880-1910. Attempts to use Chinese and Scandinavian laborers having failed, attention was focused on Italians. Estimates of Italians working in sugar parish plantations vary from 16,000 to 80,000. Most Italian agricultural workers did not remain in Louisiana. Those Italians who remained on a permanent basis worked in retail and in agriculturally related occupations. Sicilian immigrants and their progeny exhibited group cohesiveness and ethnic identity into the 20th century. See also, G.E. Cunningham, "Italians: A Hindrance to White Solidarity in Louisiana, 1890-1898." *Journal of Negro History,* vol. 50 (January 1965), pp. 22-36; and Rowland T. Berthoff, "Southern Attitudes toward Immigration, 1865-1914," *The Journal of Southern History,* vol. 17 (August 1951), pp. 328-360.

104. VILLARI, LUIGI. "Gli Italiani nel Sud degli Stati Uniti," *Bolletino dell'Emigrazione* (1907).

c. *THE MIDWEST*

105. COULTER, CHARLES W. *The Italians of Cleveland.* Cleveland: Cleveland Americanization Committee, Mayor's Advisory Committee, 1919.

106. FIORE, ALPHONSE T. *History of Italian Immigration in Nebraska.* University of Nebraska, 1942. (unpublished doctoral dissertation)

107. LA PIANA, GEORGE. *The Italians in Milwaukee, Wisconsin.* Prepared under the Direction of the Associated Charities. Milwaukee, 1915. Reprinted, San Francisco: R & E Research Associates, 1970.

108. MANFREDINI, DOLORES M. "The Italians Come to Herrin," *Illinois State Historical Society Journal,* vol. 37 (December 1944), pp. 317-328.

109. MELLONI, ALBERTO C. "Italy Invades the Bloody Third: The Early History of Milwaukee's Italians," *Milwaukee County Historical Society Historical Messenger* (March 1969), pp. 34-46.

Calls the "Mafia" imaginary.

110. [NEBRASKA] United States Federal Writers Project. *The Italians of Omaha.* Omaha: Independent Printing Co., 1941.

111. NELLI, HUMBERT S. *The Role of the "Colonial" Press in the Italian-American Community of Chicago, 1886-1921.* University of Chicago, 1965. (unpublished doctoral dissertation)

112. NELLI, HUMBERT S. *Italians in Chicago, 1880-1930: A Study in Ethnic Mobility.* New York: Oxford University Press, 1970.

"The five decades following 1880 comprised the years of major establishment, of pattern formation, of dynamic growth, and — after World War I — of group dispersion and the decline of core-area colonies. The purpose of this study is to describe and analyze the experience of Chicago's Italian community during this period." (Preface)

113. PUZZO, VIRGIL P. *The Italians in Chicago, 1890-1930.* University of Chicago, 1937. (unpublished M.A. thesis)

114. SAGER, GERTRUDE A. *Immigration: Based Upon a Study of the Italian Women and Girls of Chicago.* University of Chicago, 1914. (unpublished doctoral dissertation)

115. SCHIAVO, GIOVANNI. *The Italians in Chicago: A Study in Americanization.* Chicago: Italian American Publishing Co., 1928.

116. SCHIAVO, GIOVANNI. *The Italians in Missouri.* Chicago: Italian American Publishing Co., 1929.

117. VISMARA, JOHN C. "The Coming of the Italians to Detroit," *Michigan History Magazine,* vol. 11 (January 1918), pp. 110-124.

118. VECOLI, RUDOLPH J. *Chicago's Italians Prior to World War I: A Study of Their Social and Economic Adjustment.* University of Wisconsin, 1963. (unpublished doctoral dissertation)

See also the author's "Contadini in Chicago: A Critique of *the Uprooted,*" *Journal of American History,* vol. 51 (December 1964), pp. 404-417.

119. YOUNG, KIMBALL. *A Sociological Study of a Disintegrated Neighborhood.* University of Chicago, 1918. (unpublished M.A. thesis)

Notices of the oldest established Italian colony in Chicago.

d. *THE WEST*

120. BOHME, FREDERICK G. *A History of Italians in New Mexico.* University of New Mexico, 1958. (unpublished doctoral dissertation)

36

See the author's "The Italians in New Mexico," *New Mexico Historical Review* (April 1959), pp. 98-116.

121. DONDERO, RAYMOND. *The Italian Settlement of San Francisco Bay.* University of California, Berkeley, 1950. (unpublished M.A. thesis)

122. JONES, IDWAL. *Vines in the Sun: A Journey through California Vineyards.* New York: Ballantine, 1967 (1949).

Italians in California. See also, Andrea Sharbaro, "Wines and Vineyards of California," *Overland Monthly,* vol. 25 (January 1900), pp. 65-79; Vincent P. Carosso, *The California Wine Industry* (Berkeley: University of California Press, 1951); Mario J. Spinelli, "Italians of California," *Sunset,* vol. 14 (1904-1905), pp. 256-258; Andrew F. Rolle, "Italy in California," *Pacific Spectator,* vol. 9 (Autumn 1955), pp. 408-419; and Cleto Baroni and G.M. Tuoni, *Gente Italiana in California* (Los Angeles: L'Italo-Americano, 1928).

123. RADIN, PAUL. *The Italians of San Francisco: Their Adjustment and Acculturation.* 1935. (Monograph no. 1. Multigraphed abstract from the SERA Project 2-F2-98, 3-F2-145). Reprinted, San Francisco: R & E Research Associates, 1970.

124. ROLLE, ANDREW F. *The Immigrant Upraised. Italian Adventurers and Colonists in an Expanding America.* Norman: University of Oklahoma, 1968.

Traces the record of Italian immigrants in the American West, in some 22 states west of the Mississippi, and becomes a chronicle not only of immigrant Italian experience but equally of the multi-faceted ethnic identities out of which the American frontier and Western tradition emerged. Bibliography, pp. 351-371. Translated into Italian as *Gli Emigranti Vittoriosi* (Milan, 1972).

125. [SEATTLE] "Proud Seattle Celebration: The Citizens Pay Tribute to Their Italian Heritage," *Life,* vol. 43 (December 9, 1957), pp. 169-171.

126. SHEPPERSON, WILBUR S. "The Foreign-Born Response to Nevada," *Pacific Historical Review,* vol. 34 (February 1970), pp. 1-18.

Notices of Italians.

127. [THEATRE] *The Italian Theatre in San Francisco.* San Francisco: Works Progress Administration, 1939.

128. WALDRON, GLADYS H. *Antiforeign Movements in California, 1919-1929.* University of California, Berkeley, 1945. (unpublished doctoral dissertation)

Considerable material on Italians.

e. *CANADA*

129. ALLODI, F. "The Italians in Toronto", in W. E. Mann, ed., *Social Deviance in Canada* (Toronto: Capp Clark, 1971), pp. 250-263.

130. BELLIVEAU, J. E. "How are Canada's Italians Making Out? " *Toronto Star Magazine,* March 17, 1956.

See also, Robert T. Allen, "Portrait of Little Italy," *McLean's,* vol. 77 (1964), pp. 17-19; 43-44; 46.

131. BOISSEVAIN, J. *The Italians of Montreal: Social Adjustment in A Plural Society.* Ottawa, Canada, 1970-1971. Studies of the Royal Commission on Bilingualism and Biculturalism, No. 7.

Examines the nature of the contacts which Italians in Montreal have with Canadians of French and British origins, and the Italian's position with regard to the conflict of interests between the two dominant ethnic groups. Deals comprehensively with the origins and nature of the Italian community in Montreal. See G. Mengarelli, *Gli Italiani di Montreal* (Montreal: Centro Italiano, Attivita Commerciali Artistiche, 1957).

132. CASTELLANO, VINCENT G. *Mental Illness among Italian Immigrants.* University of Toronto, 1959. (unpublished doctoral dissertation)

133. CRAIG, JEAN C. *Associations of Persons of Italian Origin in Toronto.* University of Toronto, 1957. (unpublished doctoral dissertation).

134. FERRARIS, MARY. *Factors Influencing the Integration of a Group of Italian Women Immigrants in Toronto.* York University, 1969. (unpublished doctoral dissertation)

135. JANSEN, CLIFFORD J. "Leadership in the Toronto Italian Ethnic Group," *International Migration Review,* vol. 4 (1969), pp. 25-43.

136. JANSEN, CLIFFORD J. "The Italian Community in Toronto," in Jean L. Elliott, ed., *Immigrant Groups* (Scarborough, Ontario: Prentice-Hall, 1971), pp. 207-215.

137. SGRO, SALVATORE. *Minority Groups in the Tertiary Activity System: The Italian Presence in Metropolitan Toronto.* University of Toronto, 1972. (unpublished doctoral dissertation)

138. SIDLOFSKY, SAMUEL. *Post-War Immigrants in the Changing Metropolis with Special Reference to Toronto's Italian Population.* University of Toronto, 1969. (unpublished doctoral dissertation)

139. SPADA, A. V. *The Italians in Canada.* Ottawa: Riviera Printers, 1969.

140. ZIEGLER, SUZANNE. *The Adaptation of Italian Immigrants to Toronto: An Analysis.* York University, 1971. (unpublished doctoral dissertation)

141. ZIEGLER, SUZANNE. *Characteristics of Italian Householders in Metropolitan Toronto.* Toronto: York University, 1972. (Institute For Behavioural Research, Ethnic Research Program)

C. *MISCELLANEA*

142. AMERICAN ITALIAN HISTORICAL ASSOCIATION. Second Annual Conference. October 25, 1969 (New York City). "The Italian American Novel." *Proceedings.* Staten Island, N. Y.: American Italian Historical Association, 1970.

Conference papers by Rose B. Green, Frank Rosengarten, and Rudolph Vecoli, with panel discussion on the history and the future of the Italian-American novel. Panelists include Joseph Caruso, Ralph Corsel, Jerre Mangione, Virginia McLaughlin, and Joseph Vergara.

143. BARZIZA, DECIMUS ET ULTIMUS. *The Adventures of a Prisoner of War, 1863-1864.* Austin: University of Texas Press, 1964.

Introduction by R. Henderson Schuffler. Diary of a Confederate officer in Hood's Texas Brigade. (Son of a Venetian nobleman, married to a Virginia woman, Decimus et Ultimus was named "Tenth and Last" by his father, who could not afford any more children.)

144. BOYLE, KAY, ed. *The Autobiography of Emanuel Carnevali.* New York: Horizon, 1967.

The poet's experiences in America in the 1920's. See also Carnevali's *A Hurried Man* (Paris, 1925).

145. BRANCHI, CAMILLO E. *Il Primato degli Italiani nella Storia della Civiltà Americana.* Bologna: Zampini, 1925.

Discusses anti-Italian bigotry.

146. CAPRA, FRANK. *The Name Above the Title.* New York: Bantam Books, 1972.

Italian-American producer in Hollywood.

147. CHAPMAN, CHARLOTTE G. *Milocca: A Sicilian Village.* Cambridge, Mass.: Schenkman Publishing Co., 1971.

Study of a Sicilian village undertaken in 1928, written in 1935, and published in 1971. An in-depth view of the customs, religious beliefs, social structure and values of Milocca's inhabitants. Valuable ˙ for an understanding of the life styles of Sicilians during the period of emigration. Chapman does not use the conceptual approach of Edward C. Banfield's *The Moral Basis of a Backward Society* (New York: Free Press, 1958).

148. COMETTI, ELIZABETH, ed. and trans. *Seeing America and Its Great Men: The Journal and Letters of Count Francesco Dal Verme, 1783-1784.* Charlottesville: University of Virginia Press, 1969.

149. DICK, MARY. "Those *Americani,*" *New York Times Magazine* (April 20, 1962), p. 42.

Italians' observations on Americans in Italy.

150. GAMBINO, RICHARD. "Twenty Million Italian Americans Can't Be Wrong." *New York Times,* April 30, 1972.

A general essay, largely itself an affirmation of the resurgence of *Italianità* in the Italian-American community. For a more sophisticated affirmation of ethnic identity, see R. Vecoli, "Born Italian: Color Me Red, White and Green," *Sounding* (Spring 1973), pp. 117-123. See also, Gambino's *Blood of My Blood: The Dilemma of Italian Americans.* (N.Y.: Doubleday, 1974).

151. GIANNOTTA, ROSARIO O. *Contributions of Italians to the Development of American Culture During the Eighteenth Century.* St. John's University, 1942. (unpublished doctoral dissertation)

152. GIOVANNITTI, ARTURO. *Collected Poems.* Introduction by Norman Thomas. Chicago: E. Clemente & Sons, 1962.

The Socialist poet, and erstwhile editor of *Il Proletario.*

153. GOLINO, CARL L. "On the Italian Myth of America," *Italian Quarterly,* vol. 3 (Spring 1959), pp. 19-33.

154. GREEN, ROSE B. *The Evolution of Italian-American Fiction as a Document of the Interaction of Two Cultures.* University of Pennsylvania, 1962. (unpublished doctoral dissertation)

See the author's *The Italian-American Novel: A Document of the Interaction of Two Cultures* (Rutherford, N.J.: Fairleigh Dickinson University Press, 1974). Classifies the authors of Italian ancestry according to their responses to natural movements, analyses the structure and content of representative works, and critically evaluates the books within the framework of the established literature. Recent novels dealing with Italian-American themes include Lucas Longo, *The Family on Vendetta Street* (1968); Joe Vergara, *Love and Pasta* (1968); Ralph Corsel, *Up There the Stars* (1968); Joseph Arleo, *The Grand Street Collector* (1970); Frank Melle, *Polpetto: A Novel About Italian Americans* (1973).

155. JAFFE, IRMA B. *Joseph Stella.* Cambridge: Harvard University Press, 1970.

Joseph Stella, American painter and poet. See also, "Men and Steel: The Art of Joseph Stella," *The In-*

dependent, vol. 114 (May 9, 1925); and John I. H. Baur, "Joseph Stella," *An Exhibition at the Whitney Museum of American Art* (New York, 1963).

156. LEVI, CARLO. "Italy's Myth of America," *Life,* vol. 23 (July 7, 1947), pp. 84-86; 89-95.

157. LILIENTHAL, THEODORE W. "A Note on Gottardo Piazzoni, 1872-1945," *California Historical Society Quarterly,* vol. 38 (March 1959), pp. 7-9.

Well-known California artist.

158. LOGRASSO, ANGELINA H. "Piero Maroncelli in America," *Rassegna storica del Risorgimento,* vol. 15 (1928), pp. 894-941.

See also the author's "Poe's Piero Maroncelli," *PMLA,* vol. 55 (March 1943), pp. 780-789; "Piero Maroncelli in Philadelphia," *Romanic Review,* vol. 24 (Oct.-Dec., 1933), pp. 323-329; and *Piero Maroncelli* (Rome, 1958) for its discussion of Italian opera in the United States.

159. LOGRASSO, ANGELINA H. "Silvio Pellico in the United States," *International Comparative Literature Association, Proceedings of the Congress,* II, No. 2 (Chapel Hill: University of North Carolina, 1959), pp. 429-443.

160. LUCIANI, VINCENT. "Modern Italian Fiction in America, 1929-1954: An Annotated Bibliography of Translations," *New York Public Library Bulletin,* vol. 60 (1960), pp. 12-34.

Modern Italian literature and its impact on the American scene. See also, Sergio Pacifici, "La Riscoperta Italiana dell'America," *Quadrivio*, vol. 2 (March 1962), pp. 23-42.

161. McFADDEN, ELIZABETH. *The Glitter and the Gold: A Spirited Account of the Metropolitan Museum of Art's First Director, the Audacious and High-Handed Luigi Palma Di Cesnola.* New York; Dial Press, 1971.

Luigi Palma Di Cesnola (1832-1904), Italian born adventurer who was director of the Metropolitan Museum of Art for a quarter of a century. See also, Calvin Tomkins, *Merchants and Masterpieces: The Story of the Metropolitan Museum of Art* (New York: E. P. Dutton, 1970).

162. MANGIONE, JERRE. *Reunion in Sicily.* Boston: Little Brown, 1950.

163. MARCUSON, LEWIS R. *The Irish, the Italians and the Jews: A Study of Three Nationality Groups as Portrayed in American Drama Between 1920 and 1960.* University of Denver, 1966. (unpublished doctoral dissertation)

164. MARRARO, HOWARD R. *American Opinion on the Unification of Italy, 1846-1861.* Columbia University, 1932. Reprinted, New York: AMS Press, 1969.

See also the author's *L'Unificatione Italiana Vista dai Diplomatici Statunitensi (1848-1861),* 2 vols. (Rome, 1963-1964); and "Il Risorgimento Italiano e gli Stati Uniti," *Mondo Occidentale: Rivista bimestrale di politica e di varia cultura,* vol. 8 (April 1961), pp. 17-23.

165. MARRARO, HOWARD R. "American Studies in Italy," *South Atlantic Quarterly,* vol. 57 (Spring 1958), pp. 254-264.

See also the author's "Relazioni Culturali tra Italia e gli Stati Uniti," *Il Veltro,* vol. 4 (1960), pp. 103-112; and for Italian studies in American universities, see H. Stuart Hughes, "Gli Studi di Storia Moderna Italiana in America," *Rassegna storica del Risorgimento,* vol. 45 (April-June 1958), pp. 272-277.

166. MILLER, WAYNE. *A Gathering of Ghetto Writers: Irish, Italian, Jewish, Black, Puerto Rican.* New York: New York University Press, 1972.

Includes materials by Constantine M. Panunzio, Edward Corsi, Pietro Di Donato, John Fante, Michael De Capite, Vincent Ferrini, Thomas Del Vecchio.

167. PACE, ANTONIO. *Benjamin Franklin and Italy.* Philadelphia: American Philosophical Society, 1958.

Includes "Bibliography of Italian Frankliniana," pp. 413-439. See also, Emilio Goggio, "Benjamin Franklin and Italy," *Romanic Review,* vol. 19 (October/ December 1928), pp. 302-308.

168. PASINETTI, P. M. *From the Academy Bridge.* New York: Random House, 1970.

The two worlds of Venice and Southern California in the 1950's and 1960's. See also the author's *Smile on the Face of the Lion* (New York: Random House, 1965); and *Venetian Red* (New York: Random House, 1960).

169. PELLEGRINO, JOANNE. *In Search of Freedom: Italian Political Refugees in America, 1831-1860.* Richmond College, City University of New York, 1971. (unpublished M.A. thesis)

Among others, considers Piero Maroncelli, Frederico Canfalonieri, Giuseppe Garibaldi. "The years 1831-1860 provide valid boundaries for this work because of the great increase in emigration after 1831, and its cessation after 1860."

170. PERAGALLO, OLGA. *Italian-American Authors and their Contribution to American Literature.* New York: S. V. Vanni, 1949.

171. PETRULLO, VINCENZO. "Total War, Alien Control, and the Sicilian Community," *Annals of the American Academy of Political and Social Science,* vol. 267 (January 1950).

American G.I.'s in Sicily during World War II.

172. PREZZOLINI, GIUSEPPE. *Come gli Americani Scoprirono l'Italia, 1750-1850.* Milano: Longanesi, 1933.

American travelers in Italy, and the American image of the country.

173. PREZZOLINI, GIUSEPPE. *L'Italiano Inutile: Memorie Letterarie di Francia, Italia e America* (Milano: Longesi, 1953).

A director of the Casa Italiana (Columbia University) during the Fascist years gives his views on its affairs. See also, anonymous, "Mussolini and the Casa Italiana," *The Nation,* vol. 141 (November 27, 1935), p. 610.

174. PREZZOLINI, GIUSEPPE. "America and Italy: Myths and Realities," *Italian Quarterly,* vol. 3 (Spring 1959), pp. 3-12.

Cross cultural themes. See also the author's *America in Pantofole* (Florence, 1950); *America con gli Stivali* (Florence, 1954); *Tutta l'America* (Florence, 1958); and *I Trapiantati* (Milan, 1963).

175. ROSSI, JOSEPH. *The Image of America in Mazzini's Writings.* University of Wisconsin, 1954. (unpublished doctoral dissertation)

176. RUSSO, JOSEPH L. *Lorenzo Da Ponte, Poet and Adventurer.* Columbia University, 1922. (unpublished doctoral dissertation)

177. SOPKIN, CHARLES. "What a Tough Young Kid with *Fegataccio* Can Do on Madison Avenue," *New York Times Magazine* (January 26, 1969), pp. 32-39.

178. TORIELLI, ANDREW JOSEPH. *Italian Opinion on America as Revealed by Italian Travelers, 1850-1900.* Cambridge: Harvard University Press, 1941.

179. WARD, ROBERT J. "Europe in American Historical Romances, 1890-1910," *Midcontinent American Studies Journal* (Spring 1967), pp. 90-97.

Italians, more than other foreigners, suffered from the persistent bias of novelists.

180. WINWAR, FRANCES. *Ruotolo: Man and Artist.* New York: Harper & Row, 1949.

IV. SOCIOLOGY
OF
ITALIAN-AMERICAN LIFE

IV. SOCIOLOGY OF ITALIAN-AMERICAN LIFE

A. SOCIAL STRUCTURE: CONFLICT AND ACCULTURATION

181. ALISSI, ALBERT S. *Boys Born in Little Italy: A Comparison of their Individual Value Orientations, Family Patterns, and Peer Associations.* Western Reserve University, 1967. (unpublished doctoral dissertation)

182. AMERICAN ITALIAN HISTORICAL ASSOCIATION. Fourth Annual Conference. October 23, 1972 (New York City). "Power and Class: The Italian Experience Today." *Proceedings.* Staten Island, N. Y.: American Italian Historical Association, 1972.

    Conference papers include: F. X. Femminella and J. Scimecca, "Italian Americans and Radical Politics: An Exploratory Study of Italo-Americans on the Left"; J. Lopreato, "Social Science and Achievement Among Italian Americans"; S. M. Tomasi, "Militantism and Italian-American Unity."

183. ANGLE, PAUL M. Bloody Williamson: *A Chapter in American Lawlessness.* New York: Alfred Knopf, 1952.

    Ku Klux Klan violence against Italians.

184. APPEL, JOHN J. "American Negro and Immigrant Experience; Similarities and Differences," *American Quarterly,* vol. 18 (Spring 1966), pp. 95-103.

    Immigrant groups which have feared Black neighbors. See also, S. L. Hills, "Negroes and Immigrants in America," *Sociological Focus,* vol. 3 (Summer 1969), pp. 47-57. See also John J. Appel, *The New Immigra-*

tion (1970) which includes materials by Gino Speranza, Rocco Corresca, and Antonio Mangano. An interesting early reaction to Italian immigration is in Booker T. Washington, "Naples and the Land of the Emigrant," *The Outlook,* vol. 98 (June 1911), pp. 295-300, in which he compares Italian peasants to American Blacks. Washington maintained that Southern Italian cities had a large class living in "dirt, degradation, and ignorance at the bottom of society."

185. BAYOR, RONALD H. "Italians, Jews and Ethnic Conflict," *International Migration Review,* vol. 6 (Winter 1972), pp. 377-391.

Relationships between Jews and Italians in New York City since the 1930's. See also, Rudolf Glanz, *Jew and Italian: Historic Group Relations and the New Immigration, 1881-1924* (New York: Ktav Publishing Co., 1971), and review by R. J. Vecoli, *International Migration Review,* vol. 7 (Summer, 1973), pp. 208-209. See also, Ronald Sanders, *The Downtown Jews: Portraits of an Immigrant Generation* (New York: Harper & Row, 1969).

186. BERKSON, ISAAC B. *Theories of Americanization: A Critical Study with Special Reference to the Jewish Group.* Teachers College, Columbia University, 1920.

Published as No. 109 in Teachers College *Contributions to Education.* Important early statement with references to Italian minority community. See also, J. H. Powell, *The Concept of Cultural Pluralism in American Social Thought, 1915-1965.* (unpublished doctoral dissertation, University of Notre Dame, 1971)

187. BERNARD, WILLIAM S., ed. *Americanization Studies: The Acculturation of Immigrant Groups into American Society.* Monclair, N.J.: Patterson Smith, 1971. 10 vols.

Originally commissioned by the Carnegie Corporation and published in the 1920's. Includes: (1) Frank V. Thompson, *The Schooling of the Immigrant;* (2) John Daniels, *America Via the Neighborhood;* (3) W. I. Thomas, *Old World Traits Transplanted;* (4) Peter A. Speek, *A Stake in the Land;* (5) Michael M. Davis, *Immigrant Health and the Community;* (6) Sophonisba P. Breckinridge, *New Homes for Old;* (7) Robert E. Park, *The Immigrant Press and Its Control;* (8) John Palmer Gavit, *Americans by Choice;* (9) Kate H. Claghorn, *The Immigrants' Day in Court;* (10) William M. Leiserson, *Adjusting Immigrant and Industry.*

188. BURKE, COLIN B. "Cultural Change and the Ghetto," *Journal of Contemporary History,* vol. 4 (October 1969), pp. 173-187.

The dispersal of immigrant groups.

189. CAMPISI, PAUL J. *The Adjustment of Italian Americans to the War Crisis.* University of Chicago, 1942. (unpublished M.A. thesis)

190. CAMPISI, PAUL J. *A Scale for the Measurement of Acculturation.* University of Chicago, 1947. (unpublished doctoral dissertation)

191. CAMPISI, PAUL J. "Ethnic Family Patterns: The Italian Family in the United States," *American Journal of Sociology,* vol. 53 (May 1948), pp. 443-449.

192. CHILD, IRVIN L. *Italian or American? The Second Generation in Conflict.* New Haven: Published for the Institute of Human Relations by Yale University Press, 1943. Reissued with an introduction by F. Cordasco, New York: Russell & Russell, 1970.

Originally, Ph.D. dissertation, Yale University, 1939. A psychological approach to a general understanding of acculturation.

193. EFRON, DAVID. *Gesture and Environment. A Tentative Study of Some of the Spatio-temporal and Linguistic Aspects of the Gestural Behavior of Eastern Jews and Southern Italians in New York City, Living under Similar as well as Different Environmental Conditions.* Columbia University, 1942. (unpublished doctoral dissertation)

194. ETHNIC HERITAGE STUDIES CENTERS. Hearings before the General Subcommittee on Education of the Committee on Education and Labor. House of Representatives. 91st Congress, Second Session. On H. R. 4910. Washington: United States Government Printing Office, 1970.

See Donald G. Hohl and Michael G. Wenk, "The Rodino Bill and the Ethnic Heritage Studies Act," *International Migration Review,* vol. 7 (Summer 1973), pp. 191-194.

195. FELDMAN, EGAL. "Prostitution, the Alien Woman and the Progressive Imagination, 1910-1915," *American Quarterly,* vol. 19 (Summer 1967), pp. 192-206.

196. FERRARI, ROBERT. *Days Pleasant and Unpleasant in the Order Sons of Italy: The Problem of Race and*

Racial Societies in the United States. Assimilation or Isolation? New York: Mandy Press, 1926; Reissued with a new Foreword by F. Cordasco, Clifton, N.J.: Augustus M. Kelley, 1974.

"It is part of that ephemera churned out of the 'round-of-life' of the Italian subcommunity; and its rarity (typical of the tracts of its *genre*) is due to the short-run issue of the tract by a job printer turned publisher. . . . Ferrari helps explain the alienation [of Italian-Americans], and he affords insights which are absent in the socio-psychological portraits of outside participant-observors." (from the new *Foreword*) See also, Ernest L. Biagi, *The Purple Aster: A History of the Order Sons of Italy in America* (New York: Veritas Publishing Co., 1961); and Baldo Aquilano, *L'Ordine Figli d'Italia in America; Immigrazione Italiana, 1820-1920; Le Piccole Italie; L'Influenza Civilopolitica dell'Ordine; America ed Americanismo; La Conquista dell'Avvenire dei Figli d'Italia* (New York: Società Tipografica Italiana, 1925). See also, Ferrari's "Il Problema delle razze negli Stati Uniti con Speciale Riferimento agli Italiani," *Rivista d'Italia e d'America* (1925-1926).

197. FITZPATRICK, J. "The Experience of the Italian Neighborhood in American Society," A.C.I.M. *Symposium* (Washington, D.C., June 7, 1971).

198. GANS, HERBERT J. *The Urban Villagers: Group and Class in the Life of Italian Americans.* New York: Free Press, 1962.

Report of a participant-observation study of an inner-city Boston neighborhood, extending from October 1957 to May 1958.

199. GLAZER, NATHAN. "Ethnic Groups in America: From National Culture to Ideology," in Monroe Berger, ed., *Freedom and Control in Modern Society* (New York: 1954), pp. 158-173.

The dispersal of immigrant groups, including some notices of Italians.

200. GLAZER, NATHAN. "The Integration of American Immigrants," *Law and Contemporary Problems,* vol. 21 (Spring 1956), pp. 256-269.

On the changing problems of immigration. See also the author's "A New Look at the Melting Pot," *The Public Interest,* No. 16 (Summer 1969), pp. 180-187.

201. GLEASON, PHILIP. "The Melting Pot: Symbol of Fusion or Confusion," *American Quarterly,* vol. 16 (Spring 1964), pp. 20-46.

202. IANNI, FRANCIS A. J. *The Acculturation of the Italo-American of Norristown, Pennsylvania, 1900-1950.* Pennsylvania State University, 1952. (unpublished doctoral dissertation)

See the author's "Residential and Occupational Mobility as Indices of the Acculturation of an Ethnic Group," *Social Forces,* vol. 36 (October 1957), pp. 65-72.

203. IANNI, FRANCIS A. J. "Italo-American Teen-Ager," *Annals, American Academy of Political and Social Science,* vol. 338 (November 1961), pp. 70-78.

204. KANTROWITZ, NATHAN. "Ethnic and Racial Segregation in the New York Metropolis, 1960," *American*

Journal of Sociology, vol. 74 (May 1969), pp. 685-695.

Italians and other minority communities. See also the author's *Ethnic and Racial Segregation in the New York Metropolis* (New York: Praeger, 1973).

205. KINGSLEY, HOWARD L. and MARY CARBONE. "Attitudes of Italian-Americans Toward Race Prejudice," *Journal of Abnormal and Social Psychology,* vol. 33 (October 1938), pp. 532-537.

206. LA GUMINA, SALVATORE, ed. *Wop: A Documentary History of Anti-Italian Discrimination in the United States.* San Francisco: Straight Arrow Books, 1973.

An examination of anti-Italianism in American history; largely excerpts from periodical literature, with contemporary woodcuts and illustrations.

207. LEWIS, CHARLES A. *Communication Patterns of Recent Immigrants: A Study of Three Nationality Groups in Metropolitan Detroit.* University of Illinois, 1932. (unpublished doctoral dissertation)

Italians: pp. 32-37; 73-83; 220-225.

208. LO BELLO, NINO. *A Descriptive Analysis of Two Contiguous Ethnic Groups in New York City: A Comparative Study of the German-American Community of Ridgewood, Queens, and the Italian-American Settlement of Bushwick, Brooklyn.* New York University, 1944. (unpublished M.S. thesis)

209. McKELVEY, BLAKE. *The Emergence of Metropolitan America.* New Brunswick: Rutgers University Press, 1968.

Italians within the cultural pattern of urban America. See also the author's "The Italians of Rochester: An Historical Review," *Rochester History,* vol. 22 (October 1960), pp. 1-24.

210. MAYKOVICH, M. K. "A Comparative Study of Japanese, Italian, and Mennonite Canadians: Aspiration versus Achievement," *International Review of Sociology,* vol. I (March 1971), pp. 13-26.

Japanese and Italian Canadians fit into the Canadian value system without difficulty, although they have not been very successful in fitting into the occupational structure.

211. NELLI, HUMBERT S. "Italians in Urban America: A Study in Ethnic Adjustment," *International Migration Review,* vol. I (Summer 1967), pp. 38-55.

"Immigrant districts were responsible not for perpetuating old world traits and patterns, but for providing vital first steps in introducing newcomers into the mainstream of American life." For an autobiographical account of growing up in the Italian ghetto of Brooklyn, see Joseph N. Sorrentino, *Up From Never* (1971).

212. NOVAK, MICHAEL. *The Rise of the Unmeltable Ethnics: Politics and Culture in the Seventies.* New York: MacMillan, 1971.

See also, Peter Schrag, *The Decline of the Wasp* (New York: Simon and Schuster, 1971); and for a bibliographical critique-essay, Rudolph J. Vecoli, "European Americans: From Immigrants to Ethnics," *International Migration Review,* vol. 6 (Winter 1972), pp. 403-434. For a reaction to Novak, see R. Alter, "A Fever of Ethnicity," *Commentary,* vol. 53 (June 1972), pp. 68-73. See also, Novak's earlier essay, "White Ethnic," *Harper's Magazine,* vol. 243 (September 1971), pp. 44-50; and Vecoli, "Ethnicity: a Neglected Dimension of American History," *American Studies in Scandinavia,* vol. 4 (Summer 1970), pp. 5-23.

213. O'DONNELL, WILLIAM G. "Race Relations in a New England Town," *New England Quarterly,* vol. 14 (June 1941), pp. 235-242.

On the Italian subcommunity.

214. PALISI, BARTOLOMEO J. *Ethnicity, Family Structure, and Participation in Voluntary Associations.* University of Nebraska, 1962. (unpublished doctoral dissertation)

Based on Italian-Americans in New York. See the following articles by the author: "Ethnic Generation and Family Structure," *Journal of Marriage and Family,* vol. 28 (February 1966), pp. 49-50; "Patterns of Social Participation in a Two-Generation Sample of Italian-Americans," *Sociological Quarterly,* vol. 7 (Spring 1966), pp. 107-178; and "Ethnic Patterns of Friendship," *Phylon,* vol. 27 (Fall 1966), pp. 217-225.

215. PILEGGI, NICHOLAS. "Little Italy: Study of an Italian Ghetto," *New York,* vol. 1 (August 12, 1968), pp. 14-23.

See also the author's "How We Italians Discovered America and Kept It Pure While Giving It Lots of Singers, Judges, and Other Swell People," *Esquire,* vol. 69 (June 1968), pp. 80-82; and "The Risorgimento of Italian Power: The Red, White, and Greening of New York," *New York,* vol. 4 (June 7, 1971), pp. 26-36.

216. REED, DOROTHY. *Leisure Time of Girls in a "Little Italy."* Columbia University, 1932. (unpublished doctoral dissertation)

Comparative study of the leisure interests of adolescent girls of foreign parentage living in a metropolican community, to determine the presence or absence of interest differences in relation to behavior. See the author's published version, Portland, Oregon, 1932.

217. SMITH, JEANETTE S. "Broadcasting for Marginal Americans," *Public Opinion Quarterly,* vol. 6 (Winter 1942), pp. 588-603.

Study of discrimination against Italian-Americans.

218. SPERANZA, GINO C. *The Diary of Gino Speranza: Italy, 1915-1919.* Edited by Florence Colgate Speranza. New York: Columbia University Press, 1941. 2 vols.

Gino Charles Speranza (1872-1927), an Italian-American lawyer, paradoxically, first secretary of the Society for Italian Immigrants (incorporated in New York City in March 1901 by the reformer Sarah Wool Moore), and a restrictionist. See Gino Speranza, *Race or Nationality: A Conflict of Divided Loyalties* (Indianapolis: Bobbs, Merrill, 1925). Speranza's papers and letters are in the Manuscript Division, New York Public Library.

219. SUTTLES, GERALD D. *The Social Order of a Slum: Ethnicity and Territory in the Inner City.* Chicago: University of Chicago Press, 1968.

Italians and other minority groups. A comprehensive analysis of the internal relations of the slum area as a whole and of its links with the "extra-slum" city.

220. TOMASI, LYDIO F. *The Italian American Family: The Southern Italian American Family's Process of Adjustment to an Urban America.* New York: Center for Migration Studies, 1972.

221. TSUSHIMA, WILLIAM T. "Responses of Irish and Italians of Two Social Classes on the Marlowe-Crowne Social Desirability Scale," *Journal of Social Psychology,* vol. 77 (April 1969), pp. 215-219.

222. WHYTE, WILLIAM F. "Race Conflicts in the North End of Boston," *The New England Quarterly,* vol. 12 (December 1939), pp. 623-642.

The Boston Italian community.

223. WHYTE, WILLIAM F. *Street Corner Society: The Social Structure of an Italian Slum.* Chicago: University of Chicago Press, 1955. 2nd ed.

Revision of Ph.D. dissertation, University of Chicago, 1943. The North End, Boston Italian community.

224. WINSEY, VALENTINE ROSSELLI. *A Study of the Effect of Transplantation Upon Attitudes Toward the United States of Southern Italians in New York City as Revealed by Survivors of the Mass-Migration, 1887-1915.* New York University, 1966. (unpublished doctoral dissertation)

225. ZALOHA, ANNA. *A Study of Persistence of Italian Customs Among 143 Families of Italian Descent.* Northwestern University, 1937. (unpublished M.A. thesis)

B. *HEALTH AND RELATED CONCERNS*

226. AMERICAN ANTHROPOLOGICAL ASSOCIATION. Seventy-first Annual Meeting. November 29-December 3, 1972 (Toronto). *Proceedings.*

Conference papers include: R. M. Swiderski, "Italian American Evil Eye Charms: From Folk to Popular." Examines the traditional folk culture of Southern Italian immigrants to the United States. See M. E. Smith, "Folk Medicine Among the Sicilian-Americans of Buffalo, New York," *Urban Anthropology,* vol. 1 (Spring 1972), pp. 87-106.

227. BREMNER, ROBERT H., ed. *Children and Youth in America: Documentary History.* vol. I (1600-1865); vol. II (1866-1932: Parts 1-6; Parts 7-8). Cambridge: Harvard University Press, 1970-1971.

228. GEBHART, JOHN C. *Growth and Development of Italian Children in New York.* New York: Association for the Improvement of the Condition of the Poor, 1924.

229. LEONARD, CAROLINE W. *A Descriptive Study of the Social Settlements of East Harlem.* New York University, 1930. (unpublished M.A. thesis)

East Harlem, New York City. Extensive notices of Italian community, and its social needs.

230. LOLLI, GIORGIO, *et. al. Alcohol in Italian Culture: Food and Wine in Relation to Sobriety among Ital-*

ians and Italian-Americans. New Haven: Yale University Center of Alcohol Studies, 1958.

231. MOSELEY, DAISY H. "The Catholic Social Worker in an Italian District," *Catholic World,* vol. 114 (February 1922), pp. 618-628.

232. MOSS, LEONARD W., and WALTER H. THOMSON. "The South Italian Family: Literature and Observations," *Human Organization,* vol. 18 (Spring 1959), pp. 35-41.

233. NIZZARDINI, GENOEFFA. "Health Among the Italians in New York City," *Atlantica,* vol. 16 (December 1934), pp. 406-408, 411.

   See also the author's "Infant Mortality for Manhattan, Brooklyn, and the Bronx, 1916-1931," *Italy America Monthly,* vol. 2 (May 25, 1935), pp. 12-17.

234. QUAINTANCE, ESTHER C. *Rents and Housing Conditions in the Italian District of the Lower North Side of Chicago.* University of Chicago, 1925. (unpublished M.A. thesis)

235. ROSENWAIKE, IRA. "Two Generations of Italians in America: Their Fertility Experience," *International Migration Review,* vol. 7 (Fall 1973), pp. 271-280.

   Conclusions: "The high rates of children . . . born among Italian-born women over the age of 45 years living in the United States in 1940 are typical of women of peasant background. Their American-born daughters, however, as revealed by the 1960 census, limited their childbearing on average to levels even below those of other native Americans living in the large urban areas."

236. SANDALLS, K. F. *An Investigation of the Differential Fertility Patterns of Irish and Italian Americans.* Georgetown University, 1970. (unpublished M.A. thesis)

Catholic third-generation women of Irish origin have higher mean cumulative fertility, higher fertility ideals, and higher fertility expectations than Catholic third-generation women of Italian origin regardless of controls imposed on data of nativity, religiousness, Catholic education, or socio-economic status.

237. SPICER, DOROTHY G. "Health Superstitions of the Italian Immigrant," *Hygeia,* vol. 4 (May 1926), pp. 266-269.

238. STELLA, ANTONIO. *The Effects of Urban Congestion on Italian Women and Children.* New York: William Wood, 1908.

See also the author's "Tuberculosis and Italians in the United States," *Charities,* vol. 12 (May 7, 1904), pp. 486-489); "The Prevalence of Tuberculosis among Italians in the United States," *Transactions of the Sixth International Congress on Tuberculosis* (Washington: September 28-October 5, 1908; vols. 1-5, Philadelphia: W. F. Fell, 1908); "[Tuberculosis] among the Italians," *Charities,* vol. 21 (November 7, 1908), p. 248; *La Lotta Contro la Tuberculosi fra gli Italiani nelli Città di New York ed Effetti dell'Urbanesimo* (Roma: Tip. Colombo, 1912).

239. SWEENEY, ARTHUR. "Mental Tests for Immigrants," *North American Review,* vol. 215 (May 1922), pp. 600-612.

Objects to continuing immigration from Italy. See also Carl C. Brigham, *A Study of American Intelligence* (Princeton: Princeton University Press, 1923), for the same conclusions. On the influence of Army intelligence tests in World War I on restrictionists, see Daniel J. Kevles, "Testing the Army's Intelligence," *Journal of American History,* vol. 55 (December 1968), pp. 565-581.

240. VOGEL, EZRA. *The Marital Relationship of Parents and the Emotionally Disturbed Child.* Harvard University, 1958. (unpublished doctoral dissertation)

Some materials on the Italian family.

241. WILLIAMS, PHYLLIS H. *South Italian Folkways in Europe and America: A Handbook for Social Workers, Visiting Nurses, School Teachers, and Physicians.* New Haven: Published for the Institute of Human Relations by Yale University Press, 1938. Reissued with an introductory note by F. Cordasco, New York: Russell & Russell, 1969.

For the cultural background of the South Italian, Williams draws extensively from Giuseppe Pitrè, *Biblioteca delle Tradizioni Popolari Siciliane* (25 vols., 1871-1913). Some critical notices of Williams' work are in the review by Giovanni Schiavo, *The Vigo Review* (August 1938).

242. YOUNG, KIMBALL. *Mental Differences in Certain Immigrant Groups: Psychological Tests of South Europeans in Typical California Schools with Bearings on the Educational Policy and on the Problems of Racial*

Contacts in This Country. Leland Stanford University, 1921. (unpublished doctoral dissertation)

C. *EDUCATION*

243. ANDERSSON, THEODORE, and MILDRED BOYER. *Bilingual Schooling in the United States.* Austin, Texas: Southwest Educational Development Laboratory, 1970. 2 vols.

Includes "The Italian-Americans," II, pp. 133-146; and references to Italians in "Bibliography." See also, W. F. Mackey, *International Bibliography on Bilingualism* (Quebec: Les Presses de l'Université Laval, 1972) .which is a computer print-out of an alphabetized and indexed checklist of 11,006 titles.

244. ARSENIAN, SETH. *Bilingualism and Mental Development: A Study of the Intelligence and the Social Background of Bilingual Children in New York City.* Teachers College, Columbia University, 1937.

Published as No. 712 in Teachers College *Contributions to Education* (1937). Includes notices of Italian children.

245. BERE, MAY. *A Comparative Study of the Mental Capacity of Children of Foreign Parentage.* Teachers College, Columbia University, 1924.

Compares Italian, Jewish, and "Bohemian" children. Published as No. 154 in Teachers College *Contributions to Education* (1924).

246. BERGER, MORRIS I. *The Settlement, the Immigrant, and the Public School.* Teachers College, Columbia

University, 1956. (unpublished doctoral dissertation) Notices of Italian minority child and the public schools.

247. BERROL, SELMA C. *Immigrants at School: New York City, 1898-1914.* City University of New York, 1967. (unpublished doctoral dissertation)

Basis of author's "Immigrants at School: New York City, 1900-1910," *Urban Education,* vol. 4 (October 1969), pp. 220-230.

248. BOODY, BERTHA M. *A Psychological Study of Immigrant Children at Ellis Island.* John Hopkins University, 1924. (Ph.D. dissertation) Published, Baltimore: Williams and Wilkins, 1925.

249. *Children of Immigrants in Schools.* Vols. 29-33 of *Report of the Immigration Commission.* 41 vols. (Washington: Government Printing Office, 1911). Republished with an Introductory Essay by F. Cordasco, Metuchen, N.J.: Scarecrow Reprint Corp., 1970.

A vast depository of data on the educational background of immigrant children in America. Detailed analyses of backgrounds, nativity, school progress, and home environments of school children in 32 American cities.

250. COHEN, SOL. *Progressives and Urban School Reform: The Public Education Association of New York City, 1895-1954.* New York: Teachers College, Columbia University, 1963.

Some notices of the Italian immigrant child and the schools.

251. CORDASCO, FRANCESCO. "The Children of Immigrants in Schools: Historical Analogues of Educational Deprivation," *Journal of Negro Education,* vol. 42 (Winter 1973), pp. 44-53.

See also, Colin Greer, *The Great School Legend: A Revisionist Interpretation of American Public Education* (New York: Basic Books, 1972); and David K. Cohen, "Immigrants and Schools," *Review of Educational Research,* vol. 40 (February 1970), pp. 13-27. Also, F. Cordasco, "The School and the Children of the Poor: A Bibliography of Selected References," *Bulletin of Bibliography,* vol. 30 (July-September 1973), pp. 93-101; and F. Cordasco, "The Challenge of the Non-English Speaking Child in American Schools," *School & Society* (March 30, 1968), pp. 198-201.

252. COVELLO, LEONARD, with GUIDO D'AGOSTINO. *The Heart is the Teacher.* New York: McGraw-Hill, 1958.

Autobiography of Leonard Covello (1887-), leading American educator and longtime principal of Benjamin Franklin High School, East Harlem, New York City. Reprinted with an Introduction by F. Cordasco, *Teacher in the Urban Community: A Half-Century in City Schools* (Totowa, N.Y.: Littlefield, Adams, 1970). See also, Robert Peebles, *Leonard Covello: An Immigrant's Contribution to New York City.* New York University, 1967 (unpublished doctoral dissertation.

253. COVELLO, LEONARD. *The Social Background of the Italo-American School Child. A Study of the Southern Italian Family Mores and Their Effect on the*

School Situation in Italy and America. Edited and with an Introduction by F. Cordasco. Leiden, The Netherlands: E.J. Brill, 1967; Totowa, N.J.: Rowman and Littlefield, 1972.

Revision of Ph.D. dissertation, New York University, 1944. A major study of ethnicity, of the context of poverty, of a minority's children, and the challenges to the American school. Part I: Social Background in Italy; Part II: The Family as the Social World of the Southern Italian *Contadino* Society; Part III: Italian Family Mores and Their Educational Implications; Part IV: Summary and Conclusions.

254. FUCILLA, JOSEPH G. *The Teaching of Italian in the United States.* New Brunswick: Rutgers University Press, 1967.

A general survey. For the decline of Italian language instruction in the United States, see Herbert H. Golden, "The Teaching of Italian: The 1962 Balance Sheet," *Italica,* vol. 39 (1962), pp. 275-288. See also, Howard R. Marraro, "Doctoral Dissertations in Italian accepted by Romance Language Departments in American Universities, 1876-1950," *Bulletin of Bibliography,* vol. 20 (January-April 1951), pp. 94-99; and Mario E. Cosenza, *The Study of Italian in the United States* (New York: Italy-America Society, 1924).

255. GOGGIO, EMILIO. "Italian Educators in Early American Days," *Italica,* vol. 8 (March 1931), pp. 5-8.

See also the author's "Italian Educators in Early American Days," *Atlantica,* vol. 11 (June 1931), pp. 255-256, 281.

256. MATTHEWS, SISTER MARY FABIAN. *The Role of the Public School in the Assimilation of the Italian Immigrant Child in New York City, 1900-1914.* Fordham University, 1966. (unpublished doctoral dissertation)

"[The study] is primarily descriptive and exploratory; it is analytical to the extent to which conceptual schemes of current theories of assimilation are used to explain the Italian experience in earlier decades."

257. STANDING, E. MORTIMER. *Maria Montessori: Her Life and Work.* New York: Mentor Library, 1959.

Notices of the influence of the Italian educator-physician, Maria Montessori (1870-1952), in America. See also, Sol Cohen, "Maria Montessori: Priestess or Pedagogue?" *Teachers College Record* (Columbia University), vol. 71 (December 1969).

258. TAIT, JOSEPH W. *Some Aspects of the Effect of the Dominant American Culture Upon Children of Italian-Born Parents.* New York: Bureau of Publications, Teachers College, Columbia University, 1942; Reissued with a Foreword by F. Cordasco, Clifton, N.J.: Augustus M. Kelley, 1972.

Teachers College Contributions to Education, No. 866. Proposed to ascertain "in what direction and to what extent, if any, children, 11 to 15 years of age, of Italian born parents are affected by different amounts of contact with the dominant American culture." See also, Howard R. Weisz, *Irish-American and Italian-American Educational Views and Activities.* Columbia University, 1968. (unpublished doctoral dissertation)

259. ULIN, RICHARD O. *The Italo-American Student in the American School: A Description and Analysis of Differential Behavior.* Harvard University, 1958. (unpublished doctoral dissertation)

D. *RELIGION AND MISSIONARY WORK*

260. ABRAMSON, HAROLD J. *The Ethnic Factor in American Catholicism: An Analysis of Inter-Ethnic Marriage and Religious Involvement.* University of Chicago, 1969. (unpublished doctoral dissertation)

Includes notices of Italians.

261. AMERICAN ITALIAN HISTORICAL ASSOCIATION. Sixth Annual Conference. November 17, 1973. "The Religious Experience of Italian Americans." *Proceedings.* Staten Island, N.Y.: American Italian Historical Association, 1974.

Conference papers include: (1) S. M. Tomasi, Research in the Italian American Religious Experience; (2) E. C. Stibili, The Interest of Bishop Giovanni Battista Scalabrini of Piacenza in the "Italian Problem"; (3) R. A. Varbero, Philadelphia's South Italians and the Irish Church: A Story of Cultural Conflict; (4) H. J. Abramson, The Social Varieties of Catholic Behaviour: The Italian Experience Viewed Comparatively. Discussion of papers by D. O'Brien, W. d'Antonio, P. Kayal. Panel Discussion: Religious and Social Attitudes of Italian Americans (participants: R. Della Cara, G. Baroni, P. Di Donato, J. Groppi, N. Russo, J. Dolan.

262. CALCAGNI, CHARLES P. *A Sociological Study of the Religious Change Involving the Northern Italian in*

Barre, Vermont. (unpublished B.A. thesis, Bates College, 1954)

263. CALIARO, MARCO, and MARIO L. FRANCESCONI. *Apostolo Degli Emigranti: Giovanni Battista Scalabrini.* Milano: Editrice Ancora, 1968.

Life of Bishop Giovanni Battista Scalabrini of Piacenza who in 1887 founded the Congregation of the Missionaries of St. Charles to help Italian immigrants overseas. See also, Icilio Felici, *Father to the Immigrants: The Life of John Baptist Scalabrini* (New York: P. J. Kenedy & Sons, 1955); and G. Tessarolo, ed., *Exsul Familia: The Church's Magna Charta for Migrants* (Staten Island, New York: St. Charles Seminary, 1962).

264. CHESSA, PALMERIO. *A Survey Study of the Evangelical Work Among Italians in Chicago.* Presbyterian Theological Seminary (Chicago), 1934. (unpublished B. Div. thesis)

265. GREELEY, ANDREW M. "The Ethnic and Religious Origins of Young American Scientists and Engineers: A Research Note," *International Migration Review,* vol. 6 (Fall 1972), pp. 282-288.

Data on Italians. ("Although Italian Catholics are under-represented in all three of these broad areas of scientific enterprise, the data in Table I would suggest that, among younger scientists, Catholics are more numerous than past impressions would have led us to expect and Jews are perhaps less numerous.")

266. HACKETT, JANE K. *A Survey of Presbyterian Work with Italians in the Presbytery of Chicago.* Presby-

terian College of Christian Education, Chicago, 1943. (unpublished M.A. thesis)

267. HOFFMAN, GEORGE. *Catholic Immigrant Aid Societies in New York City from 1880 to 1920.* St. John's University, 1947. (unpublished doctoral dissertation)

Includes chapters on Italians.

268. MANGANO, ANTONIO. *Sons of Italy: A Social and Religious Study of the Italians in America.* New York: Missionary Education Movement of the United States and Canada, 1917. Reissued with a Foreword by F. Cordasco, New York: Russell & Russell, 1972.

Mangano was an Italian-American Baptist minister who served as director of the Italian department of the Colgate Theological Seminary (New York City). Other writings by Mangano include "The Effects of Emigration Upon Italy," *Charities and the Commons* (January, February, April, May, June, 1908); "Camp Schools for Immigrants," *The Immigrants in America Review* (June 1915); "The Gentle Art of Alienating Aliens," *The Immigrants in America Review* (March 1916); "Americanizing Italian Mothers," *Missions* (January 1919); "What America did for Leonardo," *World Outlook* (October 1917); "The Associated Life of the Italians in New York City," *Charities* (May 7, 1904); and *Religious Work for Italians in America: A Handbook for Leaders in Missionary Work* (New York. Immigrant Work Committee of the Home Missions Council, *c.*1915). See also, Salvatore Mondello, "Protestant Proselytism among Italians in the United States as Reported in American Magazines," *Social Science,* vol. 41 (April 1966), pp. 84-90.

269. MARSH, MAY CASE. *The Life and Work of the Churches in an Interstitial Area.* New York University, 1932. (unpublished doctoral dissertation)

Deals with social agencies in East Harlem, New York City. Extensive notices of Italian community.

270. MILESI, F. *Mons. Scalabrini e il problema dell'assistenza agli emigranti.* Università Cattolica del S. Cuore, Milano, 1965-1966. (Academic thesis)

271. MURPHY, MARY C. *Bishop Joseph Rosati, C.M., and the Diocese of New Orleans.* St. Louis University, 1961. (unpublished doctoral dissertation)

272. PALMIERI, AURELIO. *Il Grave Problema Religioso Italiano negli Stati Uniti.* Firenze, 1921.

A major work. See also, *La Società Italiana di Fronte alle Migrazioni di Massa,* a special issue of *Studi Emigrazione,* vol. 5 (Nos. 11-12), February-June 1968.

273. PICCINNI, GAETANO. *Blessed Frances Xavier Cabrini in America.* Columbia University, 1942. (unpublished M.A. thesis)

See also, Pietro Di Donato, *Immigrant Saint: The Life of Mother Cabrini* (New York: McGraw-Hill, 1960); and Theodore Maynard, *Too Small A World: The Life of Francesca Cabrini* (Milwaukee: Bruce, 1945).

274. SARTORIO, ENRICO C. *Social and Religious Life of Italians in America.* Boston: Christopher Publishing House, 1918. Reissued with a Foreword by F. Cordasco, Clifton, N.J.: Augustus M. Kelley, 1974.

One of a handful of volumes written by Italians in English on the life of Italians in the United States during the period of the great migrations. Sartorio deals with the "round-of-life" in the Italian communities; the twin dynamics of conflict and acculturation in a discussion of "Americanization"; and the role of the Churches from the viewpoint of the Protestant minister. See also Sartorio's "Work Among Italians," *The Churchman* (September 1, 1917).

275. RUSSO, NICHOLAS J. *The Religious Acculturation of the Italians in New York City.* St. John's University, 1968. (unpublished doctoral dissertation)

Indicates that three generations of American-Italians have gone through the process of absorbing the cultural patterns of American-Irish society while retaining some of their own social identity.

276. RUSSO, NICHOLAS J. "Three Generations of Italians in New York City: Their Religious Acculturation," *The International Migration Review,* vol. 3 (Spring 1969), pp. 3-17.

Appears also in Silvano M. Tomasi and Madeline H. Engel, eds., *The Italian Experience in the United States* (Staten Island: Center for Migration Studies, 1970), pp. 195-209.

277. TITUS, P. MATTHEW. *A Study of Protestant Charities in Chicago with Special Reference to Neighborhood Houses and Social Settlements.* University of Chicago, 1939. (unpublished doctoral dissertation)

Efforts among Italian immigrants.

278. TOMASI, SILVANO M. "The Ethnic Church and the Integration of Italian Immigrants in the United States," in S. M. Tomasi and M. H. Engel, eds., *The Italian Experience in the United States* (Staten Island, New York: Center for Migration Studies, 1970), pp. 163-193.

279. TOMASI, SILVANO M. *Assimilation and Religion: The Role of the Italian Ethnic Church in the New York Metropolitan Area, 1880-1930.* Fordham University, 1972. (unpublished doctoral dissertation)

An examination of the process of assimilation of Italian immigrants in the New York metropolitan area from the viewpoint of the institutional aspect of their religious experience. Data on Italian immigrants available in the archives of the dioceses of New York, Newark, Brooklyn, and Boston, as well as the General Archives of the Congregation of St. Charles (Rome), and from other sources, both Catholic and Protestant, were analyzed. Conclusions: first generation Italians created a strong community in the New York metropolitan area in the desire to preserve a continuity with the past and to find meaning and strength in their isolation, poverty, and cultural differences. The network of Italian parishes became the expression of ethnic solidarity, especially at the neighborhood level, and, to a certain degree, a strategy for coping with the surrounding society. Organized life, collective entertainment and intergroup conflict often arose and developed in a socio-religious context. Italian immigrant church leadership, clerical and lay, functioned in a mediating role between the ethnic group and the total society, beginning with the established Catholic Church.

280. VECOLI, RUDOLPH J. "Prelates and Peasants: Italian Immigrants and the Catholic Church," *Journal of Social History,* vol. 2 (Spring 1969), pp. 217-268.

281. WALSH, JOHN P. *The Catholic Church in Chicago and Problems of an Urban Society, 1893-1915.* University of Chicago, 1948. (unpublished doctoral dissertation)

Notices of Italian immigrants.

282. WILLIAMS, PHYLLIS H. *The Religious Mores of the South Italians of New Haven.* Yale University, 1933. (unpublished M.A. thesis)

E. *CRIME, DELINQUENCY & SOCIAL DEVIANCE*

283. ALBINI, JOSEPH L. *The American Mafia: Genesis of a Legend.* New York: Appleton-Century-Crofts, 1971.

A complete overview of the nature of syndicated crime in America; the genesis and development of criminal syndicates in the United States; the Italian *Mafia* and *Camorra,* and their relationships to American syndicated crime. "Looking at the present situation in syndicated crime in the United States we note that while many of its functionaries are of Italian-Sicilian and Jewish backgrounds, virtually every ethnic group is represented." Bibliography, pp. 331-348. See also, in an enormous literature, Lewis Norman, *The Honored Society: A Searching Look at the Mafia* (New York: Harper, 1964); Michele Pantaleone, *The Mafia and Politics* (New York: Coward, 1966); Paolo Sipala, "Napoleone Colajanni e Gli Studi Sulla Mafia," *Nord e Sud,* vol. 14 (No. 155, 1967), pp. 115-128; and Gordon Hawkins, "God and the Mafia," *The Public Interest,* vol. 14 (Winter 1969), pp. 24-51, a critique of Mafia literature. For an examination of popular books on the Mafia, see Murray Kempton, "The Mafia," *New York Review of Books,* vol. 13 (September 11, 1969), pp. 5-10. For historical backgrounds of urban crime and Italians, see Humbert S. Nelli, "Italians and Crime in Chicago: The Formative Years, 1890-1920," *American Journal of Sociology,* vol. 74 (January 1969), pp. 373-391; and Giovanni Schiavo, *The Truth About the Mafia and Organized Crime in America* (New York: Vigo Press, 1962).

284. AMERICAN ITALIAN HISTORICAL ASSOCIATION. Third Annual Conference. "An Inquiry into Organized Crime." October 24, 1970 (New York City). *Proceedings.* Staten Island, N.Y.: American Italian Historical Association, 1971.

Conference papers include: Francis A.J. Ianni, "A Comparative Study of Italian Secret Societies"; Pelegrini Nazzaro, "Brigantaggio, Camorra and Mafia in Italy Since the Unification"; Salvatore Mondello and Luciano J. Iorizzo, "Black Hand in Historical Perspective"; Dwight C. Smith, "The Mafia Mystique."

Panel discussion on "Mafia—Myth or Reality." Participants: Thomas J. Monahan, John Duff, Charles Grutzner, Humbert S. Nelli, Dwight C. Smith, Giulio Miranda.

285. BENNETT, WILLIAM S. "Immigrants and Crime," *Annals of the American Academy of Political and Social Science,* vol. 34 (July 1909), pp. 117-124.

Views Italians as prone to crime. See Gino C. Speranza, *et. al.,* "Crime and Immigration," *Journal of Criminal Law, Criminology, and Police Science,* vol. 4 (November 1913), pp. 523-547.

286. HALL, PRESCOTT F. "New Problems of Immigration," *Forum,* vol. 30 (1901), pp. 555-567.

Charges Italy with dumping criminals on the United States. See also, Lindsay Denison, "The Black Hand," *Everybody's Magazine,* vol. 19 (September 1908), pp. 291-301; Arthur Woods, "The Problem of the Black Hand," *McClure's Magazine,* vol. 33 (May 1909), pp. 40-47; Sydney Reid, "The Death Sign," *Independent,* vol. 70 (April 6, 1911), pp. 711-715; Cesare Lombroso, "Why Homicide has increased in the United States," *North American Review,* vol. 165 (December 1897), pp. 641-648; Gino C. Speranza, "The Mafia," *The Green Bag,* vol. 12 (June 1900), pp. 302-305; Napoleone Colajanni, "Homicide and the Italians," *Forum,* vol. 31 (March 1901), pp. 63-68; anonymous, "The Black Hand Scourge," *Cosmopolitan Magazine,* vol. 47 (June 1909), pp. 31-41. See also, Arrigo Petacco, *Joe Petrosino* (New York: Macmillan, 1974), a journalistic account of the famous New York City detective who was murdered in Palermo in 1909.

287. IANNI, FRANCIS A. J. *A Family Business: Kinship and Social Control in Organized Crime.* New York: Russell Sage Foundation, 1972.

A study of the Lupollo *Mafia* Family: "Lupollo" is the pseudonym for an Italian-American crime family which has operated in New York since the turn of the century. Conclusions: (1) There is no structured "membership" organization operating on a national level; (2) Italian-American crime families are ruled, not by fear, but by kinship; (3) concern about organized crime and the stigma of the *Mafia* has impeded the natural trend for Italian-Americans to advance in legitimate fields. See also the author's "The Mafia and the Web of Kinship," *The Public Interest* (Winter

1972), pp. 78-100; and "Formal and Social Organization in an Organized Crime 'Family': A Case Study," *University of Florida Law Review,* vol. 24 (Fall 1971). See also, Gay Talese, *Honor Thy Father* (New York: World, 1971), an account of the Bonnano family; and Mario Puzo's novel, *The Godfather* (1969), and Puzo's "The *Godfather* Business," *New York,* vol. 5 (August 21, 1972), pp. 22-29. See also, Lydio F. Tomasi, "Demythologizing Ethnic Crime," *International Migration Review,* vol. 7 (Spring 1973), pp. 72-78.

288. KOBLER, JOHN. *Capone: The Life and World of Al Capone.* New York: G. P. Putnam's Sons, 1971.

Prohibition, crime, and the Chicago underworld with Capone as central figure.

289. PANUNZIO, CONSTANTINE M. "The Foreign Born's Reaction to Prohibition," *Sociology and Social Research,* vol. 18 (January-February, 1934), pp. 223-228.

See also John R. Meers, "The California Wine and Grape Industry and Prohibition," *California Historical Society Quarterly,* vol. 46 (March 1967), pp. 19-32.

290. [SACCO-VANZETTI] Vanzetti, Bartolomeo. *Non Piangete la mia Morte: Lettere ai familiari* a cura di Cesare Pillon e Vincenzo Vanzetti. [Rome] 1962.

On the case (out of a vast literature) see: Herbert B. Ehrmann, *The Untried Case: Sacco-Vanzetti and the Morelli Gang* (New York: Vanguard, 1960), and *The Case That Will Not Die: Commonwealth vs. Sacco and Vanzetti* (Boston: Little, Brown, 1969); G. Louis Joughin and Edmund M. Morgan, *The Legacy of Sacco and Vanzetti* (Chicago: Quadrangle, 1966); Francis Russell, *Tragedy in Dedham: The Story of the Sacco and Vanzetti Case* (New York: McGraw-Hill, 1962); David Felix, *Protest: Sacco-Vanzetti: The Murder and the Myth* (New York: Devin, 1960); and Martin H. Bush, *Ben Shahn: The Passion of Sacco and Vanzetti* (Syracuse: Syracuse University Press, 1968). A brief outline of the case is in A. Dickinson, *The Sacco-Vanzetti Case* (New York: Franklin Watts, 1972).

291. SPERGEL, IRVING A. *Types of Delinquent Groups.* New York School of Social Work, 1960. (unpublished doctoral dissertation)

General backgrounds of crime in the United States, criminal syndicates, and the Mafia.

V. THE POLITICAL AND ECONOMIC CONTEXT

V. THE POLITICAL AND ECONOMIC CONTEXT

292. ALLSWANG, JOHN M. *The Political Behavior of Chicago's Ethnic Groups.* University of Pittsburgh, 1967. (unpublished doctoral dissertation)

See the author's *A House for All Peoples: Ethnic Politics in Chicago, 1890-1936* (Lexington: University of Kentucky Press, 1971). Includes a succinct commentary on the difficulties of analyzing voting behavior of "new" immigrant groups before World War I.

293. AMERICAN ITALIAN HISTORICAL ASSOCIATION. First Annual Conference. October 26, 1968 (New York City). "Ethnicity in American Political Life: The Italian American Experience." *Proceedings.* Staten Island, N.Y.: American Italian Historical Association, 1969.

Conference papers include: (1) First Session: The Political Practitioner and Ethnicity. Participants: John Cammett, Joseph F. Carlino, Alfred Santangelo, John Duff, Luciano Iorizzo. (2) Second Session: The Academician and Case Studies of Italian American Politicians. Participants: Silvano F. Tomasi, Salvatore J. La Gumina, Arthur Mann; (3) Concluding Remarks: Rudolph J. Vecoli.

294. AMERICAN ITALIAN HISTORICAL ASSOCIATION. Fifth Annual Conference. November 11, 1972 (Boston). *Proceedings.* Staten Island, N.Y.: American Italian Historical Association, 1973.

Conference papers include: J. D. Baker, "The Italian Anarchism and the American Dream: The View of John Dos Passos."

295. BAILY, SAMUEL L. "The Italians and the Development of Organized Labor in Argentina, Brazil, and the United States, 1880-1914," *Journal of Social History*, vol. 3 (Winter 1969-1970), pp. 123-134.

See also, the author's "The Italians and Organized Labor in the United States and Argentina, 1880 to 1910," *The International Migration Review*, vol. I (new series, Summer 1967), pp. 56-66.

296. BERUTTI, JOHN M. *Italo-American Diplomatic Relations, 1922-1928.* Stanford University, 1960. (unpublished doctoral dissertation)

297. BUCKLEY, TOM. "What is a Mario Procaccino," *New York Times Magazine*, August 10, 1969, pp. 7-9; 47-62.

Italian-American politician in New York City.

298. CARROLL, LEO E. "Irish and Italians in Providence, Rhode Island, 1880-1960," *Rhode Island History*, vol. 28 (August 1969), pp. 67-74.

Italian-Irish political rivalry.

299. CARTER, JOHN B. *American Reactions to Italian Fascism, 1919-1933.* Columbia University, 1953. (unpublished doctoral dissertation)

300. CLAGHORN, KATE H. *The Immigrants' Day in Court.* New York: Carnegie, 1923.

On the treatment of Italians.

301. DE CIAMPIS, MARIO. "Note sul movimento socialista tra gli emigranti Italiani negli U.S.A., 1890-1921," *Cronache Meridionale,* vol. 6 (April 1959), pp. 255-273.

302. DE SANTI, LOUIS A. *United States Relations with Italy under Mussolini, 1922-1941.* Columbia University, 1951. (unpublished doctoral dissertation)

303. DELZELL, CHARLES F. "Studi Americani sul Fascismo," *Nuovo Osservatore,* vol. 56-57 (1966), pp. 952-962.

See also, Constantine Panunzio, "Italian-Americans, Fascism and the War," *The Yale Review,* vol. 31 (June 1942), pp. 771-782; and John Norman, "Repudiation of Fascism by the Italian-American Press," *Journalism Quarterly,* vol. 21 (March 1944), pp. 1-6, 54.

304. DIGGINS, JOHN P. *Mussolini and Fascism: The View from America.* Princeton: Princeton University Press, 1972. Adapted from the author's doctoral dissertation, *Mussolini's Italy: The View from America,* University of Southern California, 1964.

Interprets the general pro-fascist attitude of most Italian Americans as an expression of ethnic pride rather than of political ideology. For opposition to Fascism, see the author's "The Italo-American Anti-Fascist Opposition," *Journal of American History,* vol. 54 (December 1967), pp. 579-598. See also, by the same author: "Flirtation with Fascism: American Pragmatic Liberals and Mussolini's Italy," *American Historical Review,* vol. 71 (January 1966), pp. 487-506;

"Mussolini and America: Hero Worship, Charisma, and the 'Vulgar Talent,'" *The Historian,* vol. 28 (August 1966), pp. 559-585; "The American Writer, Fascism, and the Liberation of Italy," *American Quarterly,* vol. 18 (Winter 1966), pp. 599-614; "American Catholics and Italian Fascism," *Journal of Contemporary History,* vol. 2 (October 1967), pp. 51-68. See also, Alan Cassels, "Fascism for Export: Italy and the United States in the Twenties," *The American Historical Review,* vol. 69 (April 1964), pp. 707-712; and William B. Smith, *The Attitude of American Catholics Toward Italian Fascism Between the Two World Wars,* Catholic University of America, 1969. (unpublished doctoral dissertation)

305. DUFF, JOHN B. "The Italians," in *The Immigrants' Influence on Wilson's Peace Policies,* ed. by Joseph P. O'Grady. Lexington: University of Kentucky Press, 1967.

306. ERIKSON, CHARLOTTE. *American Industry and the European Immigrant, 1860-1885.* Cambridge: Harvard University Press, 1957.

Italians as strikebreakers. Disproves the view that contract labor undermined the American worker.

307. FELDMAN, HERMAN. *Racial Factors in American Industry.* New York: Alfred Knopf, 1931.

Argues that "the Italian has perhaps been the most generally abused of all the foreign born." See also Gerd Korman, *Industrialization, Immigrants, and Americanizers: The View from Milwaukee, 1866-1921* (Madison: University of Wisconsin Press, 1967).

308. FENTON, EDWIN. *Immigrants and Unions, A Case Study: Italians and American Labor, 1870-1920.* Harvard University, 1957. (unpublished doctoral dissertation)

See the author's "Italians in the Labor Movement," *Pennsylvania History,* vol. 26 (April 1959), pp. 133-148; "Italian Workers in the Stone Workers Union," *Labor History,* vol. 3 (Spring 1962), pp. 188-207.

309. FERRARIS, LUIGI V. "L'Assassino di Umberto I e gli Anarchici di Paterson," *Rassegna Storica del Risorgimento,* vol. 50 (March 1968), pp. 47-64.

See also, Sidney Fine, "Anarchism and the Assassination of McKinley," *American Historical Review,* vol. 60 (July 1955), pp. 777-799; see, for background, William Preston, *Aliens and Dissenters: Federal Suppression of Radicals, 1903-1933* (Cambridge: Harvard University Press, 1963).

310. GALLO, PATRICK J. *Political Alienation Among Italians of the New York Metropolitan Region.* New York University, 1971. (unpublished doctoral dissertation)

Attempts to discern if the American political system has tended toward the integration or exclusion of ethnic groups. Sees the Italian-American as being assimilated on a number of levels but structurally unassimilated as evidenced by an occupational, residential and income differential from the core society. A structural separation results in the persistence of the Italian subsociety. Ethnicity and religion are found to be the major determinants of the perceptions of political life held by Italian-Americans on a local level. See the author's *Ethnic Alienation: The Italian-Americans* (Rutherford, N.J.: Fairleigh Dickinson University Press, 1974).

311. GERSON, LOUIS L. *The Hyphenate in Recent American Politics and Diplomacy.* Lawrence: University of Kansas Press, 1964.

See also the author's "Immigrant Groups and American Foreign Policy," *Issues and Conflicts: Studies in Twentieth Century American Diplomacy*, ed. by George L. Anderson (Lawrence: University of Kansas, 1959).

312. GIOVINCO, JOSEPH. "Democracy in Banking: The Bank of Italy and California's Italians," *California Historical Society Quarterly*, vol. 47 (September 1968), pp. 195-218.

313. GOLDBERGER, PAUL. "Tony Imperiale Stands Vigilant for Land and Order," *New York Times Magazine*, September 23, 1968, pp. 30-31, 117 ff.

Newark, N.J., Italian community, and political relationships with blacks.

314. GORDON, DANIEL N. "Immigrants and Urban Governmental Form in American Cities, 1933-1960," *American Journal of Sociology*, vol. 74 (September 1968), pp. 158-171.

Comparative notices of Italians.

315. HUTHMACHER, JOSEPH J. *Massachusetts People and*

Politics, 1919-1933. Cambridge: Harvard University Press, 1959. (unpublished doctoral dissertation)

Analyzes Italian political influences.

316. IORIZZO, LUCIANO J. *Italian Immigration and the Impact of the Padrone System.* Syracuse University, 1966. (unpublished doctoral dissertation)

See the author's "The Padrone and Immigrant Distribution," in S. M. Tomasi and M. H. Engel, eds., *The Italian Experience in the United States* (Staten Island, New York: Center for Migration Studies, 1970), pp. 43-75.

317. JAMES, MARQUIS, and BESSIE R. JAMES. *Biography of a Bank: The Story of the Bank of America* (New York: Harper, 1959).

Amadeo Pietro Giannini, the California banker. See also, Julian Dana, *Giant in the West* (1947); and Dwight L. Clarke, the Gianninis: Men of the Renaissance," *California Historical Society Quarterly,* vol. 49 (September 1970), pp. 251-269; *Ibid.,* (December 1970), pp. 337-351.

318. KARLIN, ALEXANDER J. *The Italo-American Incident of 1891.* University of Minnesota, 1941. (unpublished doctoral dissertation)

See the author's "The Italo-American Incident of 1891 and the Road to Reunion," *Journal of Southern History,* vol. 8 (May 1942), pp. 242-246; "The New Orleans Lynching of 1891 and the American Press," *Louisiana Historical Quarterly,* vol. 24 (1941), pp. 187-204; "Some Repercussions of the New Orleans

Mafia Incident of 1891," *Research Studies of the State College of Washington* (Pullman, Washington), vol. 11 (December 1943), pp. 267-282.

319. KERN, PAUL J. "Fiorello La Guardia," in John Salter, ed., *The American Politician* (Chapel Hill: University of North Carolina Press, 1938), pp. 3-46.

320. LA GUMINA, SALVATORE J. *Vito Marcantonio, Labor and the New Deal, 1935-1940.* St. John's University, 1966. (unpublished doctoral dissertation)

East Harlem (New York City) political leader, Vito Marcantonio (1902-1954). Published as *Vito Marcantonio* (Dubuque, Iowa: Kendall-Hunt, 1969). See further the author's "Ethnic Groups in the New York Elections of 1970," *New York History,* vol. 53 (January 1972), pp. 55-71; and "The New Deal, the Immigrants and Congressman Vito Marcantonio," *International Migration Review,* vol. 4 (Spring 1970), pp. 57-75.

321. LEVY, MARK R., and MICHAEL S. KRAMER. *The Ethnic Factor: How America's Minorities Decide Elections.* New York: Simon & Schuster, 1972.

Notices of Italian-American electorate.

322. MANN, ARTHUR. *La Guardia, A Fighter Against His Times, 1882-1933.* Chicago: University of Chicago Press, 1969.

See also the author's *La Guardia Comes to Power, 1933* (Philadelphia: Lippincott, 1965).

323. MELTZER, MILTON. *Bread And Roses: The Struggle*

of American Labor, 1865-1915. New York: Knopf, 1967.

The Italian community and the Lawrence, Massachusetts, textile mill strike of 1912. See also, Donald B. Cole, *Immigrant City: Lawrence, Massachusetts, 1845-1921* (Chapel Hill: University of North Carolina Press, 1963).

324. NELLI, HUMBERT. "The Italian Padrone System in the United States," *Labor History,* vol. 5 (Spring 1964), pp. 153-167.

See also, Marie Lipari, "The Padrone System: An Aspect of American Economic History," *Italy-American Monthly,* vol. 2 (April 1935), pp. 4-10.

325. NELLI, HUMBERT S. "John Powers and the Italians: Politics in a Chicago Ward, 1896-1921," *Journal of American History,* vol. 57 (June 1970), pp. 67-84.

Italian-Irish political rivalry.

326. NORMAN, JOHN. *Italo-American Opinion in the Ethiopian Crisis: A Study of Fascist Propaganda.* Clark University, 1942. (unpublished doctoral dissertation)

327. ODENCRANTZ, LOUISE C. *Italian Women in Industry: A Study of Conditions in New York City.* New York: Russell sage Foundation, 1919. Reissued with a Foreword by F. Cordasco, Clifton, N.J.: Augustus M. Kelley, 1974.

Period of the study is 1911-1913, and the area studied was "the lower end of Manhattan, below Fourteenth Street, which includes several Italian neighborhoods."

Included in the study were 1,095 Italian women wage earners.

328. PARENTI, MICHAEL J. *Ethnic and Political Attitudes: A Depth Study of Italian Americans.* Yale University, 1962. (unpublished doctoral dissertation)

Predicts the passing of ethnic loyalties and "balanced" tickets. See also the author's "Ethnic Politics and the Persistence of Ethnic Identification," *American Political Science Review,* vol. 56 (September 1967), pp. 717-726.

329. PFAU, JAMES. *Economic Relations Between the United States and Italy, 1919-1949.* University of Chicago, 1951. (unpublished doctoral dissertation)

330. POSNER, RUSSELL M. "The Bank of Italy and the 1926 Campaign in California," *California Historical Society of Southern California Quarterly,* vol. 39 (June 1957), pp. 190-201.

331. ROSSI, ERNEST E. *The United States and the 1948 Italian Election.* University of Pittsburgh, 1964. (unpublished doctoral dissertation)

332. SCHAFFER, ALAN. *Caucus in a Phone Booth: The Congressional Career of Vito Marcantonio, 1934-1950.* University of Virginia, 1962. (Ph.D. dissertation)

Study of East Harlem (New York City) political leader, Vito Marcantonio (1902-1954). Published as *Vito Marcantonio: Radical in Congress* (Syracuse: Syracuse University Press, 1966). See also, Annette T. Rubinstein, ed., *Vito Marcantonio: Debates, Speech-*

es, and Writings, 1935-1950 (New York: Vito Marcantonio Memorial Fund, 1956; Reissued with a Foreword by F. Cordasco, Totowa, N.J.: Augustus M. Kelley, 1973).

333. SPERANZA, GINO C. "The Alien in Relation to our
Laws," *American Academy of Political and Social
Science,* vol. 51 (March 1914), pp. 169-176.

334. TRESCA, CARLO. *Autobiography* [Manuscript Section, New York Public Library.]

Unpublished Ms of Carlo Tresca, founder and editor
of the anarchist newspaper *Il Martello.* See also, John
Dos Passos, "Carlo Tresca," *Nation,* vol. 159 (January
23, 1943), p. 123; and Max Eastman, "Profile:
Troublemaker," *New Yorker,* vol. 10 (September 15,
1934), p. 31. For early material on Italian anarchists,
see Paul Ghio, *L'Anarchisme aux Etats Unis* (Paris:
Colin, 1903).

335. WEED, PERRY L. *The White Ethnic Movement and
Ethnic Politics.* New York: Praeger, 1973.

Includes "Italian-Americans and Joseph Colombo,"
pp. 51-62. See also, Lawrence H. Fuchs, ed., *American Ethnic Politics* (New York: Harper & Row,
1968); and Samuel T. McSeveney, "Ethnic Groups,
Ethnic Conflicts, and Recent Quantitative Research
in American Political History," *International Migration Review,* vol. 7 (Spring 1973), pp. 14-33.

336. WENK, MICHAEL S., S. M. TOMASI, and GENO
BARONI. *Pieces of a Dream: The Ethnic Worker's
Crisis with America.* New York: Center for Migration
Studies, 1972.

337. WOODY, ROBERT H. "The Labor and Immigration Problem of South Carolina during Reconstruction," *Mississippi Valley Historical Review,* vol. 18 (September 1931), pp. 196-202.

Early efforts to attract Italian labor. On attempts to replace Negroes with Italian agricultural workers, see Robert L. Brandfon, "The End of Immigration to the Cotton Fields," *The Mississippi Valley Historical Review,* vol. 50 (March 1964), pp. 591-611.

338. ZINN, HOWARD. *Fiorello La Guardia in Congress.* Columbia University, 1958. (unpublished doctoral dissertation)

APPENDIX:
CASA ITALIANA EDUCATIONAL
BUREAU PUBLICATIONS

The
Casa Italiana Educational Bureau

Its Purpose and Program

by

LEONARD COVELLO

●

Bulletin Number 4

CASA ITALIANA EDUCATIONAL BUREAU

Columbia University, New York City

The

CASA ITALIANA EDUCATIONAL BUREAU

Its Purpose and Program

•

IMMIGRATION always creates problems which have their origin in the fundamental one of the transition of cultures and the inevitable conflict attendant thereupon. Assimilation, even by a homogenous people, gives rise to a measure of disruption and disorganization. America was created, built up, and is today the result of successive waves of immigration from many countries and dissimilar peoples. If it had been a truly homogenous and integrated nation, the problems which confronted former immigrant groups and which face the Italian community today would not have assumed such great proportions.

It is estimated that in New York City those of Italian origin number well over a million. Of this number almost a half million were born in Italy. In short, the Italian-American group is still essentially an immigrant group. On the basis of the above figures, we must realize that the Italian population of New York City naturally must present many problems of adjustment to this new environment. These problems are inherent in the situation. This condition prevails, altho perhaps not so acutely, wherever there are Italians in this country.

Italian immigration, in its early phases was temporary in character. In the main, the early arrivals were not seeking to establish permanent residence. Only during the last quarter of a century has the Italian community taken root in American soil. Today, however, it can definitely be said that Italian Americans are reaching forth in every direction in their desire to "belong" and to participate in American life.

Where the Italian immigrant is concerned, the assimilative process has been retarded partly because of lack of intelligent handling on the part of the larger American community and partly by the Italian community itself.

The American community could not, or would not, see the problems that were being created. It is also reasonable to conclude that the Italian, because he considered himself a transient, failed to become conscious of his broader social responsibilities. There was no real development of an immigrant community—it was rather an agglomeration of numerous disjointed groupings. The genius for leadership, which the Italian has exercised thru the ages was given little chance to express itself. Wholesome social forces within the groups were never integrated to a common program of ministering to the varied needs of an immigrant people.

The need for unification and coordination of all kinds of educational work in Italian-American communities is therefore a pressing matter. The policy of drifting and of short-sighted opportunism has been all too dominant in shaping the direction of Italian-American community life. The urgent need for some central educational organization has been felt, recognized, discussed, wished for, and longed for on the part of a great many social-minded individuals of Italian origin and others who have understood the significance of the question. In this report on the need for and purpose of the Bureau, we cannot treat this matter as fully as it deserves to be treated. We shall return to this argument in subsequent bulletins because we feel not enough intelligent public discussion has taken place on this very vital subject.

With this situation in mind the Casa Italiana Educational Bureau was organized in May, 1932.

The purposes of the Bureau may be listed under three categories:

1. The Bureau will be a *fact finding* organization. Its purpose is to gather and present social and educational facts for all agencies and individuals to whom such information may be of interest and value.

2. The Bureau will serve as a medium for *centralization of efforts* directed toward social and cultural advancement of the Italian American.

3. The Bureau will formulate and initiate a *promotional* program of educational and social activities. To this end it will concern itself with the establishment and guidance of similar organizations thruout the United States.

WHAT THE BUREAU HAS BEEN DOING:

Until very recently the Bureau has purposely centered its efforts in laying a sound foundation for the larger aspects of its work.

1. The Italian Language. The Bureau considers the teaching of the Italian language one of the strongest educational forces in the Italian-American community. The language assumes this importance because of its cultural value in American life and its social significance in the Italian-American community.

With this in view the Bureau has undertaken an educational campaign for the diffusion of the Italian language by utilizing the educational elements in the Italian communities, as well as those elements in American life that show a desire to cooperate in this movement.

2. Reference and Research.

(a) *A Study of the Italian Population in New York City.*

Basic to an understanding of its problems is the necessity of discovering exactly where the Italian population in New York City is located, what types of neighborhoods are inhabited by Italians, and the social and economic status of the Italian population. A statistical analysis of the trend of mobility and change in the Italian population in New York City between 1916 and 1931 is being made. This will be supplemented by community and individual case studies.

(b) *A Study of the Disintegrating and Disruptive Forces* in the Italian-American communities of New York City has been projected in order to deal more intelligently and more adequately with such serious symptoms as retardation, truancy, and juvenile delinquency.

(c) *Italian Language Press in the United States.* The Bureau is studying the attitudes, interests, and activities of Italian Americans as expressed in the columns of the Italian language newspapers.

(d) The Bureau is compiling a comprehensive list of *reference material* as well as a *bibliography* on immigration and problems created by the immigrant in America with special reference to the Italian group.

3. A speakers' group, under the direction of Miss Annita E. Giacobbe, is now in process of organization. The speakers' group, which will soon function, will concern itself with Italian-American educational problems and will be at the service of any cultural or educational organization.

* * *

As can be seen, the Casa Italiana Educational Bureau now exists in fact. It has been functioning for a year and a half, in spite of very limited resources. Professor Giuseppe Prezzolini, Director of the Casa Italiana, has not only sponsored the project but has given it a home. The Emergency Work Bureau and the Works Division of the Department of Public Welfare, New York City, have provided it with competent workers, without whom it would have been practically impossible to make any headway in the research program. This branch of the work, planned by the Executive Director, assisted by Mr. Irving Sollins and Mr. Jay Beck, Director of the Research Division, is being carried on under the direction of Mr. Jay Beck, with the valuable assistance of Mr. William B. Shedd, Statistician for the Bureau. The Bureau has received cooperation from many sources. Public and private organizations as well as individuals have given freely of advice and assistance.

To carry on its work effectively and to exercise its potentialities as an organ of constructive and beneficial activities, as outlined herein, it is necessary that the Bureau be given the full support of every American of Italian origin and of all others who may be interested in its aims and work. With the assurance of such support, the Casa Italiana Educational Bureau will be in a position to render continuous, valuable public service and, we hope, to achieve lasting and far reaching results.

LEONARD COVELLO, Executive Director
Casa Italiana Educational Bureau.

The Italians in America

A Brief Survey of a Sociological Research
Program of Italo-American
Communities

(With two Population Maps and a Table)

By

LEONARD COVELLO

Bulletin Number 6

—

Casa Italiana Educational Bureau

—

Columbia University, New York City

FOREWORD

There are almost 5,000,000 Italians of the first and second generations in the United States. They, therefore, represent, numerically as well as culturally, an important national minority group.

The Italian communities in the United States are still immigrant communities, with all the problems that confront such communities. The Casa Italiana Educational Bureau is preparing studies on the Italo-American communities in order to evaluate the character of the cultural changes which are constantly in process in these communities.

The Bureau represents the first efforts for a comprehensive program of research and educational guidance for these communities. The location of these communities, their numerical strength, their social and cultural development are matters of vital concern to all of us—Italian and non-Italian. The Bureau is also concerned with creating and developing good will and understanding of these communities by the larger American community.

The Casa Italiana Educational Bureau was organized because of a feeling that direct and practical results could be realized by a concentration of effort in this direction.

LEONARD COVELLO, *Executive Director*

Casa Italiana Educational Bureau

THE ITALIANS IN AMERICA

—

About a half year ago we pointed out elswhere the urgent
need for coordination of all kinds of social and educational work
in Italian American communities. We suggested at that time
the importance of an integrated program, ministering to the varied needs of an immigrant people and to the descendants of an
immigrant people. This program was to be based not upon a
disjointed agglomeration of opinions and prejudices concerning
the Italian American; not upon a lack of knowledge; not upon a
short-sighted and opportunistic purpose. Rather, the services to
be rendered were to be unified into an objectively conceived, practical and dynamic program.

It is this planning—or the approach to the plan which we
wish to develop here, very briefly and concisely in the short space
allotted to us. In the future, we shall go into a more explicit and
detailed analysis of each phase of our work. What we present
now is merely an outline of what can be done and what remains to
be done.

* * *

Before any plan can be worked out intelligently certain
fundamentals are absolutely necessary. There is needed the indispensable fact-finding concerning the Italian American and the
Italian American community. This process of gathering authentic
information must be scientific and objective. The efforts to obtain
this information must be centralized to avoid duplication. For this
there should be a competent organization, interested primarily in
an unbiased approach to the problems that it plans to tackle. It
must then enlist the aid and cooperation of all the experts who are
interested in the problems of the Italian American and of all the
educational and social institutions in New York City, elsewhere

in the United States, and in Italy. What is more—in offering its services—educational, fact-finding, promoting Italian language and culture, facilitating the adjustment of the Italian American to his life in this country—it must interest Italian American students, particularly those pursuing graduate work, in the much needed studies of these problems and of their solution.

In being authentic, objective and scientific, the approach to these problems must also consider the attitude and viewpoint of the Italian American. Probably he alone can approach the problem with a keen and sympathetic understanding; feel more immediately the urgent necessity of such study; sense most intimately the perplexities that confront his own people—for he, himself, is undergoing or has undergone the processes of adjustment to the American scene.

This function the Casa Italiana Educational Bureau intends to fulfill by endeavoring to give direction to wholesome social and educational forces for the Italian American community.

Surprising as it may seem, the fact is that there has been no such organization. Since there is no organized and unified Italian community in this country, how can we speak authoritatively as being a centralizing factor in the development of such a community?

Our answer is that we fully realize that only upon the basis of the results of our work will such recognition be accorded us. We feel that these results will justify and gain the recognition, support and cooperation of the Italian American people. Already through the auspices of this Bureau—for the first time in the history of the Italian colony of New York—over 250 independent societies, lodges and affiliations of national organizations in New York City and vicinity were brought together during the past season to support a definite educational program which resulted, among other things, in the establishment of a permanent fund for scholarships for American students of Italian origin.

Our immediate efforts are focussed on the problems in New York City and its environs, where there is the greatest concentration of Italian immigrant population in the United States. With the proper backing, and if its endeavors prove to be worthwhile here, the Bureau will willingly cooperate with and offer its services to all Italian American communities in a consulting capacity.

This brings us to another point—our function in a consulting capacity. It was in this capacity that we realized the dearth of real knowledge and the need for such knowledge. During our very brief existence we have been consulted time and again by various organizations and individuals, Italian 'and non-Italian, for data concerning the Italian population. Educators, teachers and students have secured material and references from us to facilitate their programs for inter-group relations between various immigrant groups and the native population. We have been asked for data concerning the Italian contributions to Western civilization in general and to America in particular. We have supplied information to students of the problems that directly affect the Italian American groups and individuals. We have made available to them the sources of information relating to these problems.

Competent students should be interested in such problems as:

1. The Italian American background — social, political, economic.

2. The history of Italian migrations and in particular Italian immigration to the United States.

3. The adjustment of the Italian to American life and the problems involved; causes of maladjustment; attempted solutions; processes of Americanization at work in the Italian American community.

Of course, all these studies are broad and general in nature. We indicate here, in brief outline, specific studies, some of which we have been working on, and some of which are merely projected for the future.

RESEARCH PROJECTS
(Studies in Process)

I. **Study of Natural Areas of Italians in New York City.**

　1. Spotting by residence: Marriages, Births, Deaths for 1916 and 1931.

　2. Spotting of schools, churches, health centers, recreational centers, libraries, etc., in Italian communities.

　3. 15th U. S. Census—1930. Distribution of 1st and 2nd generation Italians by Health Areas.

II. **Demographic Statistics of Italians in New York City.**

　A. Analysis of Material on Marriage, Birth and Death Schedules.　(Copied from original records of Department of Health, N. Y. C.)

　1. Marriage Schedule:
　　a. Correlation between ages of groom and bride.
　　b. Occupation of groom.
　　c. Intermarriage of first generation Italian.
　　d. Propinquity of residence.

　2. Birth Schedule:
　　a. Nativity of each parent.
　　b. Father's occupation.
　　c. Number of children born and number of children living according to age and nativity of mother.

　3. Death Schedule:
　　a. Nativity of deceased.
　　b. Age distribution.
　　c. Nativity of each parent.
　　d. Occupation.
　　e. Cause of Death.

　B. A Study of Marriage and Intermarriage of Second

Generation of Italian Americans.
Source: Marriage License Bureau.

III. **Community Case Studies in New York City.**

Source: An old established Italian community and a new community in the Bronx. One existing in 1916 and another developed since 1916.

1. Physical condition of streets and houses.
2. Rentals.
3. Recreational facilities.
4. Educational facilities.
5. Civic development and interest.
6. Health.
7. Standard of living.
8. Delinquency and crime.
9. Individual and family case studies.

IV. **Padrone System.**

An historical account of the Padrone System in America; its social consequences; the economic conditions which made its existence possible; and an appraisal of the contributions of the immigrant, especially the Italian to our economic development.

V. **Italian Societies.**

A study of their growth and development and their influence on the Italian American.

VI. **Study of Italian Social and Educational Backgrounds in Italy**

Source: 800 cases through Geography Schedule.

VII. **Study of Language Factor in Italian Homes.**

Source: Language Questionnaire given at a New York City high school to students of Italian origin.

VIII. **Italian Language Press in United States.**

Studies of attitudes, interests and activities of Italian Americans with particular emphasis on Metropolitan New York.

a. Analysis of 150 newspapers and periodicals in the Italian language in United States.

b. Clippings from New York City newspapers in the Italian language. (classified under 24 main subject headings).

IX. Juvenile Delinquency 1916 and 1931.
Source: Children's Court, New York City.

1. Spotting of residence for all arraignments.
2. Spotting of Italian arraignments.
3. Analysis:
a. Comparison of Italians with total group according to offense, age, nativity of child and parents.
b. Recidivism.
c. Tendency to offend singly or in groups.

X. Neglect.
(*Improper Guardianship and Control of Children*).
Source: Children's Court, New York City.

1. Spotting of residence.
2. Correlation with other available data.

XI. Police Attitudes and Their Effect Upon the Italian American.
Source: Interviews with Police and members of the group studied.

XII. Reference Material.
References indexed by topic, indicating sources of published material on immigration and social problems inherent in a large foreign population, such as

a. Housing.
b. Crime and Delinquency.
c. Mental Ability.
d. Conflicts in Customs and Mores.
e. Intermarriage.
f. Assimilation Problems, etc.

XIII. Annotated Bibliography.

1. Italians in America.
   a. Books on immigration and problems created by the immigrant in America with special reference to the Italian group.
2. Italian emigration and Italians in America with viewpoint of Italian writers and observers.
3. Italian emigration and Italians in America with viewpoint of non-Italian writers and observers.

XIV. Community Studies of Italians in United States.

Studies of Italian Community Units, i. e., groups which have come from the same town or village in Italy and have retained partial unity as communities in America.

1. Riberese in United States.
2. Aviglianese in United States.
3. Other groups—if material can be secured.

Studies of Italian-American Community or Communities which have been formed in America.

1. New London, Connecticut.
2. Westerly, Rhode Island.
3. Endicott, New York.
4. Tarrytown, New York.
5. Scranton, Pennsylvania.
6. Montclair, New Jersey.
7. Monroe, New York.

Above studies to be based on outline "Cultural Changes in Italian-American Communities," by Miss Florence G. Cassidy.

XV. Study of Professional Groups of Italian Origin in N. Y. C.

1. Teachers of Italian origin in New York City.
2. Physicians of Italian origin in New York City.
   a. Training (Italy or United States).
   b. Office location.

c. Hospital connections.
d. Specialty.
e. Nationality of Clientele.
3. Other occupational groups where access to material makes study feasible.

XVI. Italian Press (In Italy).

Studies of attitudes in Italy toward America, American Institutions, the Italian American and Italian-American relations with an evaluation of the potential and active influence on the Italian American.

Source: Italy's leading newspapers.

XVII. Truancy.

Sources: Reports from School Principals to the Bureau of Reference and Research, New York City.

In the aforementioned work and projected plans, practical advice and access to necessary data have been given by the Department of Health of New York City, the Police Department, Board of Education, Children's Court and the Welfare Council. Likewise the library at Teachers' College, the other libraries at Columbia University, the Russell Sage Library, and the New York Public Library have been of great assistance.

We have also availed ourselves of the wide experience and expert knowledge of a number of consultants who have given us freely of their time and advice. They are men and women who are outstanding in their respective fields: Florence G. Cassidy, Secretary, National Institute of Immigrant Welfare; Robert E. Chaddock, Professor of Statistics, Columbia University; Hon. Edward Corsi, Director Home Relief, New York City; Frederick E. Croxton, Assistant Professor of Statistics, Columbia University; Robert Ferrari, Professor of Contracts and of Criminology, John Marshall College of Law; Corrado Gini, Professor of Statistics, University of Rome, Italy; Dr. George W. Kirchwey, Head of Department of Criminology, New York School of Social Work;

Walter W. Pettit, Assistant Director, New York School of Social Work; Dr. Nathan Peyser, Principal P. S. 181, Brooklyn; Sophia M. Robison, Research Bureau, Welfare Council; Dr. Frederic M. Thrasher, Associate Professor of Educational Sociology, New York University; Bessie B. Wessel, Professor of Sociology, Connecticut College for Women.

Since the Bureau's existence, the workers have been provided by the Emergency Work Bureau and the Civil Works Service. The Works Division of the Department of Public Welfare is continuing to make possible our work on its present scale.

The type of work we have outlined has in recent years been recognized to be of utmost importance by sociologists and educators. The problem of sound adjustment to the American scene cannot be solved without study and conscious direction from social and educational agencies.

It should be mentioned, however, that securing authentic information concerning specific immigrant groups is not a simple matter. There is the resistance engendered among officials in public and private agencies because of the attitude against identifying the various immigrant stocks as hyphenates. Statistical information, for instance, is incomplete. Those organizations, who supposedly have the information, have not collected their data nor interpreted it from the veiwpoint of the specific Italian American problems, or for that matter from the viewpoint of the definite problems of any nationality group. The United States decennial census is becoming increasingly helpful but its data is still incomplete. The immigration records up to recent times were deficient in many respects. The Casa Italiana Educational Bureau, as a recognized body interested in these specific problems hopes to assist in improving official and private attitudes so that more complete statistical and other pertinent information may be secured and made available for responsible educational bodies.

Those multitudinous factors which complicate the assimilative process must be studied not merely externally but also internally, from the viewpoint of those who are making these adjustments. Opposition may often arise from the immigrant community itself, due, in part, to the attitude of superiority and antagonism of the native American. But this resistance can easily be avoided by having investigators who are Italian Americans themselves, or who possess a sympathetic and intimate understanding of the psychology and of the background and mores of the Italian.

The study of any immigrant population in a particular part of the United States should show the relation of that part to the rest of that immigrant population in this country. The two maps and the chart that we present here will clearly show the number and distribution of the Italian stock (first and second generations) in the United States.

Map I.—Distribution of Italians in the United States.

Map II.—Six contiguous Eastern states containing 72.9 per cent of the total Italian stock in the United States.

Table I.—Cities having 5,000 Italian Americans and over.

In conclusion, we are eager to add that suggestions and information from all the Italian communities in the United States will be welcomed. We seek intimate cooperation with them. We wish to gauge their approval or disapproval of our plan and of our projected studies. What particularly are the specific problems that face the American of Italian extraction? What authentic information have they as to the history of the Italian community from its very beginnings down to this very day? What sociological and historical studies pertaining to the Italian American as an individual or as a member of the community do they think should be made? As an educational and research body, it will be only by the close cooperation of the Italian American community, and with the various agencies and learned bodies of this country that the Casa Italiana Educational Bureau may be able to work out a sound and complete picture, showing all the ramifications of the role, life and position of the Italian American in the United States.

LEONARD COVELLO
Executive Director
July, 1934. *Casa Italiana Educational Bureau.*

MAP OF UNITED STATES
⤙ POPULATION OF ITALIAN ORIGIN ⤚
1ˢᵗ & 2ⁿᵈ GENERATIONS
FROM 15ᵀᴴ U.S. CENSUS 1930

PREPARED BY
·CASA ITALIANA EDUCATIONAL BUREAU·
·COLUMBIA UNIVERSITY·
MAY 1934

·LEGEND·

● 1,000,000 ITALIANS
◆ 100,000 "
● 10,000 "
○ 1,000 "

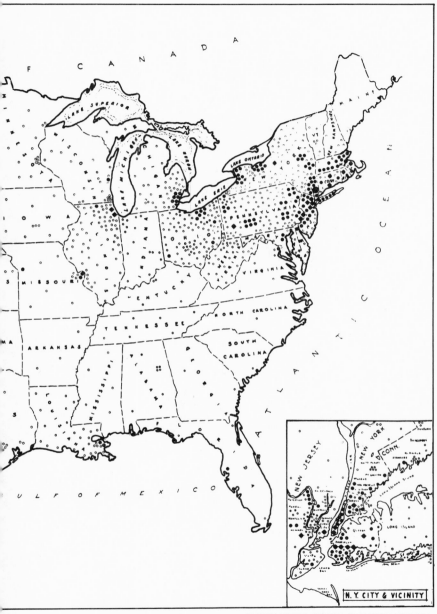

① FROM "ITALY AMERICA MONTHLY," JULY 1934.

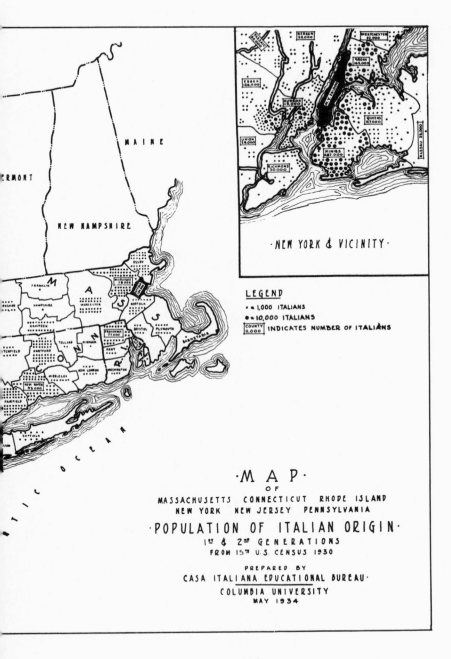

·MAP·
OF
MASSACHUSETTS   CONNECTICUT   RHODE ISLAND
NEW YORK   NEW JERSEY   PENNSYLVANIA
·POPULATION OF ITALIAN ORIGIN·
1ˢᵗ & 2ⁿᵈ GENERATIONS
FROM 15ᵀᴴ U.S. CENSUS 1930

PREPARED BY
CASA ITALIANA EDUCATIONAL BUREAU·
COLUMBIA UNIVERSITY
MAY 1934

STATE	FOREIGN BORN ITALIANS	NATIVE ITALIANS OF ITALIAN PARENTAGE	TOTAL ITALIANS	TOTAL POPULATION	PERCENTAGE OF ITALIANS TO TOTAL POPULATION
ALABAMA	2,140	4,446	6,586	2,646,248	.249
ARIZONA	822	1,285	2,107	435,573	.484
ARKANSAS	952	1,947	2,899	1,854,482	.156
CALIFORNIA	107,249	129,373	236,622	5,677,251	4.162
COLORADO	10,670	20,683	31,353	1,035,791	3.027
CONNECTICUT	87,123	140,139	227,262	1,606,903	14.143
DELAWARE	3,769	6,516	10,285	238,380	4.314
DIS. of COLUMBIA WASHINGTON	4,330	5,840	10,170	486,869	2.088
FLORIDA	5,262	8,053	13,315	1,468,211	.907
GEORGIA	712	1,005	1,717	2,900,506	.590
IDAHO	1,153	1,584	2,737	445,032	.615
ILLINOIS	110,449	161,040	271,489	7,630,654	3.556
INDIANA	6,873	9,663	16,536	3,328,503	.510
IOWA	3,834	5,913	9,747	2,470,939	.394
KANSAS	2,165	3,662	5,827	1,880,999	.010
KENTUCKY	1,509	2,964	4,353	2,614,589	.174
LOUISIANA	13,526	34,912	48,438	2,101,593	2.304
MAINE	2,359	4,109	6,468	797,423	.811
MARYLAND	10,872	17,465	28,357	1,631,526	1.737
MASSACHUSETTS	126,103	196,573	322,676	4,249,614	7.593
MICHIGAN	43,087	54,961	98,048	4,842,325	2.025
MINNESOTA	6,401	10,774	17,175	2,563,953	.670
MISSISSIPPI	1,613	3,403	5,016	2,009,821	.249
MISSOURI	15,204	24,111	39,315	3,629,367	1.083
MONTANA	2,840	3,485	6,325	537,606	1.176
NEBRASKA	3,642	5,347	8,989	1,377,963	.652

CITY	STATE	NUMBER OF ITALIANS	TOTAL POPULATION	PERCENTAGE OF ITALIANS TO TOTAL POPULATION
N.Y. CITY	N.Y.	1,070,355	6,930,446	15.444
PHILADELPHIA	PA.	182,368	1,950,961	9.346
CHICAGO	ILL.	181,861	3,376,438	5.306
BOSTON	MASS.	90,819	781,188	11.625
NEWARK	N.J.	85,598	442,337	19.306
DETROIT	MICH.	61,968	1,568,662	3.950
SAN FRANCISCO	CAL.	58,021	634,394	9.146
CLEVELAND	OHIO	36,317	900,429	6.254
ROCHESTER	N.Y.	55,413	328,132	16.887
PROVIDENCE	R.I.	53,635	252,981	21.201
BUFFALO	N.Y.	51,361	573,076	8.962
PITTSBURGH	PA.	47,940	669,817	7.157
JERSEY CITY	N.J.	44,914	316,715	14.181
NEW HAVEN	CONN.	41,658	162,655	25.734
LOS ANGELES	CAL.	29,545	1,238,048	2.386
PATERSON	N.J.	29,333	138,513	21.180
NEW ORLEANS	LA.	24,011	458,762	5.234
ST. LOUIS	MO.	23,817	821,960	2.897
BALTIMORE	MD.	23,305	804,874	2.900
BRIDGEPORT	CONN.	21,837	146,716	14.884
SYRACUSE	N.Y.	21,702	209,326	10.367
UTICA	N.Y.	21,091	101,740	20.730
HARTFORD	CONN.	20,986	164,072	12.791
TRENTON	N.J.	19,284	123,356	15.633
YONKERS	N.Y.	17,306	134,646	12.853
LAWRENCE	MASS.	15,106	85,068	17.757

CITY	STATE	NUMBER OF ITALIANS	TOTAL POPULATION	PERCENTAGE OF ITALIANS TO TOTAL POPULATION
DENVER	COL.	9,071	287,861	3.151
NEW BRITAIN	CONN.	9,043	68,128	13.273
NORTH BERGEN	N.J.	8,968	40,714	22.027
REVERE	MASS.	8,966	35,680	25.129
DAYONNE	N.J.	8,777	88,979	9.864
CAMBRIDGE	MASS.	8,595	113,643	7.563
W.NEW YORK	N.J.	8,565	37,107	23.135
ORANGE	N.J.	8,467	35,599	23.919
GARFIELD	N.J.	8,363	29,739	28.121
ERIE	PA.	8,357	115,967	7.206
WILMINGTON	DEL.	8,346	106,597	7.829
NEW CASTLE	PA.	8,318	48,674	17.089
YOUNGSTOWN	OHIO	8,088	170,002	4.757
OMAHA	NEB.	7,862	214,006	3.674
MEDFORD	MASS.	7,672	59,714	12.846
PORT CHESTER	N.Y.	7,662	22,662	33.810
PASSAIC	N.J.	7,654	62,959	12.157
SEATTLE	WASH.	7,441	365,583	2.035
CINCINNATI	OHIO	7,432	451,160	1.647
QUINCY	MASS.	7,421	71,983	10.310
ROCKFORD	ILL.	7,368	85,864	8.581
HAZELTON	PA.	7,346	36,765	19.980
ROME	N.Y.	6,981	32,330	21.507
COLUMBUS	OHIO	6,918	290,564	2.381
LODI	N.J.	6,899	11,549	59.737
BELLEVILLE	N.J.	6,867	26,974	25.578

DISTRIBUTION IN UNITED STATES OF ITALIAN POPULATION BY STATES

NEW JERSEY	190,858	316,322	507,180	4,041,334	12,550
NEW MEXICO	1,259	2,118	3,377	423,317	.798
NEW YORK	629,322	923,147	1,552,469	12,588,066	12,333
N.CAROLINA	438	710	1,148	3,170,276	.362
N DAKOTA	102	170	272	680,845	.399
OHIO	71,496	108,956	180,452	6,646,697	2.715
OKLAHOMA	1,157	2,270	3,427	2,396,040	.143
OREGON	4,728	5,141	9,869	953,786	1.035
PENNSYLVANIA	225,979	307,778	613,257	9,631,350	6.367
RHODE ISLAND	32,493	59,543	92,036	687,497	13.587
S.CAROLINA	168	473	611	1,738,765	.351
S DAKOTA	305	536	841	692,849	1.714
TENNESSEE	1,946	3,689	5,635	2,616,556	.215
TEXAS	6,550	15,101	21,651	5,824,715	.371
UTAH	2,814	4,166	6,980	507,847	1.374
VERMONT	3,082	4,485	7,567	359,611	2.104
VIRGINIA	1,853	3,643	5,496	2,421,051	.227
WASHINGTON	10,274	12,098	22,372	1,563,396	1.431
W VIRGINIA	12,088	20,102	32,190	1,729,205	1.861
WISCONSIN	12,599	19,538	32,137	2,939,006	1.094
WYOMING	1,653	2,084	3,737	225,565	1.656
TOTAL	1,790,424	2,756,453	4,546,877	122,775,046	3.703

ITALIAN STOCK OF 1ST AND 2ND GENERATIONS OVER 5000 IN PRINCIPAL CITIES OF UNITED STATES

SCHENECTADY	N.Y.	14,233	95,629	14,874
NIAGARA FALLS	N.Y.	13,000	75,460	17,227
SOMERVILLE	MASS	12,846	102,908	12,365
MILWAUKEE	WIS	17,444	578,249	2.152
WORCESTER	MASS	12,341	195,311	6.316
SPRINGFIELD	MASS	12,095	149,900	8.060
MT.VERNON	N.Y.	12,068	61,499	19,623
ELIZABETH	N.J.	11,217	114,589	9.789
SCRANTON	PA	10,775	143,433	7.512
SAN JOSE	CAL	10,650	57,651	18,473
AKRON	OHIO	10,398	255,040	4.077
WASHINGTON	D.C.	10,170	486,869	2.088
STAMFORD	CONN	10,062	46,346	21,753
KANSAS CITY	MO.	9,341	399,746	2.486
ALBANY	N.Y.	9,642	127,412	7.567
NEW ROCHELLE	N.Y.	9,345	54,000	17,305
EVERETT	MASS.	9,212	40,424	19,024
CRANSTON	R.I.	9,190	42,911	21,416
PORTLAND	ORE	6,429	301,815	2.130
TORRINGTON	CONN	6,160	26,040	23,656
PITTSTON	PA.	6,107	62?,017	.911
MILFORD	PA.	6,024	14,741	40,866
READING	PA.	5,914	111,171	5.319
CHICAGO HGTS	ILL.	5,899	22,321	26,428
CANTON	OHIO	5,725	104,906	5.457
DUNMORE	PA.	5,679	22,627	25,096
KENOSHA	WIS	5,643	50,262	11,267
NEWTON	MASS	5,536	65,276	8.461
AMSTERDAM	N.Y.	5,494	34,817	15,779
PITTSFIELD	MASS	5,469	49,677	11,009
ALTOONA	PA.	5,447	82,054	6.638
AUBURN	N.Y.	5,386	36,652	14,646
HACKENSACK	N.J.	5,276	24,568	21,475
LYNN	MASS	5,248	102,320	5.129
SACRAMENTO	CAL.	5,197	93,750	5.543
NORWALK	CONN.	5,046	36,019	14,065

PREPARED BY
CASA ITALIANA EDUCATIONAL BUREAU
COLUMBIA UNIVERSITY
MAY 1934
Source - 15th U.S. Census - 1930

Italian Population in New York

By

WILLIAM B. SHEDD

Bulletin Number 7

CASA ITALIANA EDUCATIONAL BUREAU

Columbia University, New York City

FOREWORD

●

One of the major functions of the Casa Italiana Educational Bureau is to study the social life of the Italian and his adjustment to his new environment in the United States.

Intelligent planning for social and educational needs of a community depends largely upon research and investigation, which give the basic social data of the community in question. Population studies, involving death and birth rates, age distribution, vocational and occupational adjustments, extent of delinquency, trends in marriage, etc. are the basic elements for any social or educational studies that may be needed. It is only when this authentic data—this source material—has been gathered and analyzed that intelligent and forward-looking educational and social programs are possible.

The following article, one of a series which is being published in bulletin form by the Casa Italiana Educational Bureau, offers this basic information. Mr. William B. Shedd, statistician of the Bureau, presents a brief report of the population of Italian origin in New York City. As far as we know this is the first time that such an analysis has been made for the Italians in New York City.

Leonard Covello, Executive Director
Casa Italiana Educational Bureau

ACKNOWLEDGEMENT:

The writer wishes to acknowledge his indebtedness to Professor Robert E. Chaddock, Professor Frederick E. Croxton, Mr. Leonard Covello, and Mr. Jay Beck for their valuable suggestions throughout the course of this study; to the Neighborhood Statistics Division, Research Bureau, Welfare Council, for its cooperation in making available for transcription material in the 15th U. S. Census tally sheets for New York City. In fairness to them, it should be stated that such statements and conclusions as are made are the writer's.

The Works Division of the Department of Public Welfare, New York City, by its generous assistance in providing competent workers for the Casa Italiana Educational Bureau, has made this study possible.

William B. Shedd.

Italian Population
in
New York

By WILLIAM B. SHEDD,*

● Groups, from the beginning of time, have found it necessary to count their numbers. Historically, taxation and military considerations were probably the primary reasons for taking censuses. Accurate counts were also necessary to determine representation in legislative bodies. In recent years health and social agencies have found accurate definition and description of their problems absolutely necessary for checking their work and for intelligent planning for the future. The proper location of schools, public works, and social agencies depends, in part, upon a knowledge of the particular population which each is to serve. Without the census, the New York City Department of Health would be unable to compute birth, death and disease rates which are indispensable guides in public health work. As a matter of fact, the use of the census by these agencies has become so great that there is pressure to conduct a census counting in 1935 and every five years thereafter, instead of in ten-year intervals as heretofore.

The material for any particular immigrant group cannot be found in any place except the original census tally sheets, because of the prohibitive cost of compiling and publishing a detailed comprehensive nationality survey by small geographic areas. If an organization wishes to obtain facts concerning such a group, it must, at its own expense, select and transcribe them from the original Census tally sheets. The Casa Italiana Educational Bureau has been able to obtain this material through the cooperation of the Welfare Council of New York City which acted as temporary custodian for the 1930 Census sheets in New York City.

For purposes of the Census, New York City is divided into over 3,000 divisions called Census Tracts or Sanitary Districts. Each of these has an area of about 40 acres (approximately 10 city blocks). All the facts and data collected by census enumerators are first tabulated for each Tract. They are entered on Tally Sheets and the results are then added up and finally arranged by boroughs. The totals for the boroughs can be found in the volumes of the United States Census. The data given by Tracts is very detailed and, because of their great number, unwieldy. To simplify this for the purpose of the Department, in 1928 the New York City Department of Health, which had also used the Sanitary District as a statistical unit, created a new unit called the Health Area. Each Health Area contained about 25,000 people living under similar social and economic conditions. This homogeneity however, has not been maintained during the few years that the Health Area has been used as a measuring unit. Despite this, its increasing use makes it a most practical statistical unit for all types of social studies for New York City.

ITALIAN AREAS
IN NEW YORK CITY

Italians have been coming in numbers to this country for about half a century. The Federal government, during this period, has made no less than five census enumerations. Of these, only the recent census of 1930 provides any material concerning second-generation population of Italian origin which can be used as an adequate basis for social studies. Even this does not fully meet the requirements of those interested in a thorough study of Italian population in the United States. However, such material as is available and certain conclusions which can be drawn from it will be presented here.

The first detailed tabulation of Italian-born and their children[1] in New York City is contained in Table 1 (number and Proportion of persons of Italian Parentage, by Health Areas).

---

[1] In this article reference is made to first, second and third generation Italians; The customary basis of classification is as follows:
1. First generation Italians—the Italian immigrant.
2. Second generation—The child born in the United States of parents whose nativity is as follows:
    (a) One parent born in Italy, other parent born in United States:
    (b) Both parents foreign-born, but father is born in Italy. This includes the case where both parents are born in Italy.
3. Third generation—Child born in United States, one or both of whose parents were second generation Italians.

THE ITALIAN OF THE
THIRD GENERATION

The question now arises: To what extent do these figures represent *all* those of Italian origin? In other words, how many third-generation Italians (who are listed in the census as native white of native parentage) are there? In studying the Italian population we are a great deal more fortunate than those dealing with groups of other national origins, because the bulk of Italian immigration did not get under way until about thirty years or a little more than one generation ago. This leads us to believe that the third generation Italians are comparatively few in number. A glance at the figures of nativity composition for selected Health Areas, which are overwhelmingly Italian, and at the age figures available for four of these areas, would seem to bear out this conclusion. In Health Area 11, Bronx, (South of Bronx Park), with 81% Italians; Health Areas 21 and 22, Manhattan (in East Harlem), with respectively 80% and 79% Italians; and Health Area 82,

Brooklyn (in Bensonhurst), with 70% Italians, (See Table II. Column 1), the class of native-white of native parentage makes up only a very small percentage of the total. This in itself proves nothing, but the age distribution (See Table III) by nativity classes, i.e., first and second generations of foreign stock, in the same selected Health Areas, shows that while the first-generation group is essentially older and the second-generation group is younger, the group of native white of native parentage in which are found those of third generation is overwhelmingly a young age group in that at least 55% of the total in this group in each Area is under fourteen years of age. Since there are few native-white of native parentage in the older age class, it follows that the parents of the children in these Areas must come from the other possible group, that is the second generation of foreign stock. This group, as we have seen, in these two Areas is mostly Italian. All this would tend to show that as yet third-generation Italians do not make up a great proportion of the Italian population. However, we have no way of checking on Italians in those Areas where they are in a minority as we have in the Areas which are predominantly Italian. It may be that one of the

factors to explain this is that with the coming of these third-generation children many Italians moved out of the neighborhood.

AGE DISTRIBUTION*
OF ITALIANS

A knowledge of the age distribution of the population is essential in all social studies. Without it, birth and death statistics are worse than meaningless; they may be misleading. Juvenile delinquency and crime figures may lead to unwarranted conclusions without knowledge of the age distribution which makes up the particular population that is being studied. A graphic example of misleading conclusions which may result from disregarding the age distribution factor occurred during the Philippine Insurrection. Many charges were made of the deplorable state of health in the American army at this time. The report, made to answer those charges, stated that conditions were not entirely as they should be, but that they were no worse than the conditions in large American cities. Figures were produced by army officials which showed that the death rates for the army and for the city of Boston were about the same. It is obvious that the conclusion drawn from this comparison was false and invalid, because a city containing old, infirm people and infants is a great deal more susceptible to death from natural causes than a group of young army men who normally contribute least to the general death rate.

There are no census figures available on the age distribution of Italians, because they have been included with groups of other national origins under the headings of Foreign-born White and Native White of Foreign Parentage, as shown in Table III. We therefore, can only make a general statement about age distribution of Italians

in New York City, which will be reinforced by such evidence as we have available. Several attempts were made to show a relationship between the number of Italians in each Health Area and each age class of the total population in that Area.

This was to determine whether the percentage of the total population for any particular age class increases or decreases as the percentage of Italians in the Area increases. While these attempts produced no results which would enable us to show a detailed Italian age distribution, they do give positive indications that the first and second generation Italian in New York City is definitely in a younger age class than the general population.

Table IV gives the percentage under and over 21 years in several Manhattan Health Areas, chosen because their population was predominantly of selected national origins. It can be seen that the population of the Italian Health Areas is almost evenly divided between the two age classes while the Jewish, Irish and German Areas have populations which have definite tendencies to mass toward the older ages. **Since Italians are a later immigrant group, it is to be expected that they would tend toward the younger ages more than the other groups. The reason for this is that immigrant groups are usually made up of young and middle aged people and only the passing of time can counterbalance this conscious selection. Table V gives comparisons of the age distribution of the total population in four predominantly Italian Health Areas with that of the** total population in each of the respective boroughs. It is seen that the Italian Health Areas have a greater concentration in the younger age classes than the entire boroughs have. And since the Italians make up part of the age distribution of the total population of the borough, it follows, that to counterbalance the influence of the Italians, there are other groups which have even less in the younger ages than are indicated in the total borough distribution. Thus, we can assume that there is an even greater disparity between age distribution of Italians and the rest of New York's population than is shown in Table V.

According to the United States Census of 1930,[3] there were 4,546,788 Italians of first and second generations in the United States, of whom 1,070,-355—roughly one-fourth—were living in New York City.

Because of that fact, this city becomes a fruitful field for the further study of this group. Not only are there concentrated communities here, but there exist educational institutions, welfare organizations, and other types of facilities, public and private, which make a planned investigation into many of the phases of the Italian community feasible. However, until the age composition of this population of Italian origin is better known, statements about the condition of Italian health, delinquency, and similar social phenomena can be only general and for the most part unsubstantiated.

[2] The ages of the members that make up a population group such as the Italian group vary from infancy to extreme old age. In an age distribution, individuals are grouped in certain specific age classes from lowest to highest, which are useful for describing a population for particular purposes, e. g. school attendance, juvenile delinquency, industrial employment, old age retirement, child bearing, etc. The age divisions which we have adopted for our studies are:

birth—5 years	35 years—44 years
5 years—14 years	45 years—64 years
15 years—24 years	65 years and over.
25 years—34 years	

A more detailed distribution in the early ages, under 25 years, is, of course, more generally useful.

[3] See article "The Italians in America" by Leonard Covello, Casa Italiana Educational Bureau, Bulletin No. 6.

Column (1) gives the number of the Health Area.

Column (2) gives the Total Population in the Area.

Column (3) gives the Total Italian population, i. e., first and second generation Italians.

Column (4) gives the percentage of total Italian population to the entire population in the Area.

Column (5) gives the number in the Area born in Italy, i. e., the first-generation Italians.

Column (6) gives the percentage of Italian-born to the total Italian population, i. e., the proportion that the first generation bears to the total Italian population as given in Column (3).

Column (7) gives the number of native-born children of first generation Italians, i. e., second-generation Italians.

It can be seen that in a few Areas, a large proportion of the total population is of Italian origin. On the other hand, in most of the Areas, there is only a small percentage of Italians. Examination of Table I and Map I, will show that there are concentrations of Italians in fairly well defined Areas, which we can call Natural Areas, as distinguished from the formal areas, such as Census Tracts, Police Districts, Assembly Districts, etc.

Table I—A: NUMBER AND PROPORTION OF PERSONS OF ITALIAN PARENTAGE,
BY HEALTH AREAS, MANHATTAN, NEW YORK CITY, 1930

(First and second generations)

Health Area (1)	Total Population (2)	Total Italian 1st & 2nd Generation (3)	% Total Italians in Total Population (4)	Foreign Born or 1st Generation Italians (5)	% Foreign Born in Total Italian Population (6)	Native Born or 2nd Generation Italians (7)
Total	1,867,312	260,702	13.96	117,740	45.2	142,962
1	33,839	1,343	4.0	518	38.6	825
2.10	23,786	1,382	5.8	592	42.8	790
2.20	28,576	671	2.3	294	43.8	377
3	25,820	364	1.4	146	40.1	218
4	30,952	1,353	4.4	604	44.6	749
5	26,370	842	3.2	377	44.8	465
6	31,664	760	2.4	338	44.5	422
7	33,691	602	1.8	252	41.9	350
8	30,412	80	.3	40	50.0	40
9	24,853	490	2.0	238	48.6	252
10	28,593	39	.1	17	43.6	22
11	22,673	1,065	4.7	453	42.5	612
12	23,863	184	.8	98	53.3	86
13	24,359	15	.1	5	33.3	10
14	19,333	744	3.8	334	44.9	410
15	22,068	440	2.0	243	55.2	197
41	21,960	586	2.7	118	20.1	468
42	23,329	3,529	15.1	1,545	43.8	1,984
43	21,619	805	3.7	348	43.2	457
44	13,758	663	4.8	292	44.0	371
45	11,767	943	8.0	444	47.1	499
46	14,594	569	3.9	281	49.4	288
47	36,626	2,459	6.7	1,380	56.1	1,079
48	28,698	691	2.4	385	55.7	306
49	20,248	5,277	26.1	2,594	49.2	2,683
50	16,237	3,375	20.8	1,725	51.1	1,650
51	24,258	4,951	20.4	2,894	58.5	2,057
52	19,590	1,707	8.7	1,041	61.0	666
53	16,662	594	3.6	296	49.8	298
54	17,518	2,128	12.1	1,062	49.9	1,066
55	21,580	5,123	23.7	2,891	56.4	2,232
56	26,342	1,665	6.3	901	54.1	764

16	27,252	1,638	6.0	681	41.6	957	57	23,616	8,138	34.5	4,001	49.2	4,137
17	24,356	11,453	47.0	4,560	39.8	6,893	58	21,742	5,397	24.8	2,647	49.0	2,750
18	25,048	445	1.8	222	49.9	223	59	14,255	2,847	20.0	1,408	49.5	1,439
19	24,810	234	.9	108	46.2	126	60	17,114	4,415	25.8	2,121	48.0	2,294
20	30,696	3,657	11.9	1,715	46.9	1,942	61	15,226	1,389	9.1	720	51.8	669
21	15,659	12,465	79.6	5,005	40.2	7,460	62	26,076	11,372	43.6	5,616	49.4	5,756
22	25,962	20,399	78.6	8,117	39.8	12,282	63	14,621	1,068	7.3	480	44.9	588
23	34,785	714	2.1	344	48.2	370	64	23,943	8,796	36.7	4,450	50.6	4,346
24	24,472	433	1.8	260	60.0	173	65	15,609	4,026	25.8	1,845	45.8	2,181
25	26,586	5,691	21.4	2,489	43.7	3,202	66	14,732	1,396	9.5	638	45.7	758
26	18,314	15,439	84.3	6,623	42.9	8,816	67	23,529	369	1.6	148	40.1	221
27	36,907	1,688	4.6	792	46.9	896	68	14,779	10,195	69.0	4,250	41.7	5,945
28	21,468	547	2.5	237	43.3	310	69	20,814	18,353	88.2	7,345	40.0	11,008
29	25,589	2,662	10.4	1,125	42.3	1,537	70	13,459	6,048	44.9	2,860	47.3	3,188
30	17,518	5,805	33.1	2,453	42.3	3,352	71	16,938	1,515	8.9	721	47.6	794
31	38,653	338	.9	149	44.1	189	72	15,259	585	3.8	232	39.7	353
32	33,843	858	2.5	454	52.9	404	73	12,524	257	2.1	120	46.7	137
33	21,222	2,245	10.6	1,039	46.3	1,206	74	14,757	3,145	21.3	1,698	54.0	1,447
34	22,017	266	1.2	135	50.8	131	75	20,589	3,136	15.2	1,511	48.2	1,625
35	26,738	592	2.2	330	55.7	262	76	15,953	2,379	14.9	929	39.1	1,450
36	32,853	509	1.5	243	47.7	266	77	26,279	7,583	28.9	3,089	40.7	4,494
37	23,906	1,354	5.7	563	41.6	791	78	21,923	13,486	61.5	5,926	43.9	7,560
38	22,088	935	4.2	400	42.8	535	79	14,047	2,442	17.4	1,131	46.3	1,311
39	22,576	3,394	15.0	1,503	44.3	1,891	80	17,992	998	5.5	369	37.0	629
40	22,632	665	2.9	362	54.4	303	81	19,948	1,502	7.5	830	55.3	672

See map on pages 162-163.

Table I—B: NUMBER AND PROPORTION OF PERSONS OF ITALIAN PARENTAGE,
BY HEALTH AREAS, BROOKLYN, NEW YORK CITY, 1930

(First and second generations)

Health Area (1)	Total Population (2)	Total Italian 1st & 2nd Generation Population (3)	% Total Italians in Total Population (4)	Foreign Born or 1st Generation Italians (5)	% Foreign Born in Total Italian Population (6)	Native Born or 2nd Generation Italian. (7)
Total	2,560,401	487,344	19.03	193,435	39.7	293,909
1	20,518	1,101	5.4	441	40.1	660
2	23,006	2,633	11.4	821	31.2	1,812
3	17,860	754	4.2	268	35.5	486
4	21,265	1,616	7.6	581	36.0	1,035
5	31,924	1,291	4.0	522	40.4	769
6	31,920	1,931	6.0	821	42.5	1,110
7	28,110	16,682	59.3	5,837	35.0	10,845
8	18,776	11,378	60.6	4,525	39.8	6,853
9	20,941	8,871	42.4	3,141	35.4	5,730
10	18,147	6,771	37.3	2,577	38.1	4,194
11	15,620	8,728	55.9	3,249	37.2	5,479
12	21,472	2,976	13.9	1,081	36.3	1,895
13	23,709	2,935	12.4	993	33.8	1,942
14	29,642	16,505	55.7	6,282	38.1	10,223
15	18,634	4,248	22.8	1,975	46.5	2,273
16	18,198	3,121	17.2	1,381	44.2	1,740
17	23,311	7,242	31.1	3,137	43.3	4,105
18	22,525	2,136	9.5	833	39.0	1,303
19	23,503	2,205	9.4	838	38.0	1,367
20	22,341	1,488	6.7	578	38.8	910
21	19,010	1,279	6.7	495	38.7	784

Health Area (1)	Total Population (2)	Total Italian 1st & 2nd Generation (3)	% Total Italians in Total Population (4)	Foreign Born or 1st Generation Italians (5)	% Foreign Born in Total Italian Population (6)	Native Born or 2nd Generation Italians (7)
54	24,998	2,056	8.2	805	39.2	1,251
55.10	23,627	1,537	6.5	547	35.6	990
55.20	28,368	2,523	8.9	938	37.2	1,585
56	24,860	120	.5	41	34.2	79
57	23,357	4,023	17.2	1,558	38.7	2,465
58.10	25,584	192	.8	61	31.8	131
58.20	24,105	107	.4	51	47.7	56
59	25,710	392	1.5	160	40.8	232
60	22,793	579	2.5	223	38.5	356
61	27,290	1,788	6.6	768	43.0	1,020
62	30,160	7,350	24.4	2,796	38.0	4,554
63	29,040	141	.5	61	43.3	80
64.10	15,423	5,475	35.5	2,045	37.4	3,430
64.20	22,681	3,016	13.3	1,124	37.3	1,892
64.30	160	49	30.0	22	44.9	27
65	28,321	2,475	8.7	966	39.0	1,509
66	30,970	4,048	13.1	1,698	41.9	2,350
67	35,924	5,123	14.3	1,925	37.6	3,198
68	26,554	4,352	16.4	1,724	39.6	2,628
69	26,862	7,349	27.4	2,870	39.1	4,479
70	27,642	2,564	9.3	918	35.8	1,646
71.10	13,268	1,274	9.6	495	38.9	779

22	18,188	10,048	55.2	4,407	43.9	5,641
23	30,033	1,771	5.9	712	40.2	1,059
24	20,861	3,567	17.1	1,347	37.8	2,220
25	15,102	6,471	42.8	2,482	38.4	3,989
26	21,707	2,389	11.0	984	41.2	1,405
27	36,769	6,299	17.1	2,258	35.8	4,041
28	25,044	1,290	5.2	488	37.8	802
29	29,390	1,017	3.5	373	36.7	644
30	26,676	1,545	5.8	595	38.5	950
31	26,542	5,348	20.1	2,021	37.8	3,327
32	26,007	11,402	43.8	5,274	46.3	6,128
33	29,511	8,214	27.8	3,629	44.2	4,585
34	28,436	5,258	18.5	2,269	43.2	2,989
35	26,408	2,603	9.9	1,095	42.1	1,508
36	19,593	5,710	29.1	2,074	36.3	3,636
37	14,571	9,358	64.2	3,442	36.8	5,916
38	23,991	5,193	21.6	1,910	36.8	3,283
39	23,928	1,302	5.4	481	36.9	821
40	30,411	21,398	70.4	9,842	46.0	11,556
41	27,707	11,842	42.7	4,784	40.4	7,058
42	23,031	13,372	58.1	5,029	37.6	8,343
43	16,662	4,929	29.6	1,875	38.0	3,054
44	21,403	9,178	42.9	3,757	40.9	5,421
45	25,053	1,178	4.7	442	37.5	736
46	25,466	2,406	9.4	876	36.4	1,530
47	29,477	5,856	19.9	2,153	36.8	3,703
48	30,413	4,569	15.0	1,471	32.2	3,098
49	28,263	628	2.2	161	25.6	467
50	39,489	1,642	4.2	601	36.6	1,041
51	26,093	684	2.6	255	37.3	429
52	18,059	2,253	12.5	808	35.9	1,445
53.10	17,102	2,356	13.8	850	36.1	1,506
53.20	23,057	404	1.8	134	33.2	270
71.20	24,790	2,221	9.0	851	38.3	1,370
72.10	26,357	747	2.8	279	37.3	468
72.20	12,067	383	3.2	128	33.4	255
73.10	23,551	1,009	4.3	363	36.0	646
73.20	17,824	1,190	6.7	449	37.7	741
74.10	26,637	1,852	7.2	654	35.3	1,198
74.20	7,768	1,363	17.5	515	37.8	848
75.10	12,706	4,494	35.4	1,766	39.3	2,728
75.20	14,253	2,202	15.4	901	40.9	1,301
76	28,223	1,872	6.6	728	38.9	1,144
77	22,480	1,785	7.9	699	39.2	1,086
78.10	22,722	2,241	9.9	835	37.3	1,406
78.20	11,219	3,383	30.2	1,298	38.4	2,085
79	37,668	4,957	13.2	1,835	37.0	3,122
80.10	20,716	13,966	67.4	5,461	39.1	8,505
80.20	14,527	8,498	58.5	3,293	38.8	5,205
81.10	18,912	5,749	30.4	2,275	39.6	3,474
81.20	22,094	8,885	40.2	3,956	44.5	4,929
82	30,887	21,613	70.0	9,101	42.1	12,512
83	33,286	3,692	11.1	1,537	41.6	2,155
84	26,241	6,112	23.3	2,871	47.0	3,241
85.10	26,116	4,414	16.9	1,777	40.3	2,637
85.20	30,354	8,004	26.4	3,524	44.0	4,480
86.10	21,081	13,071	62.0	5,563	42.6	7,508
86.20	23,402	12,210	52.2	5,012	41.0	7,198
87.10	18,621	2,068	11.1	791	38.2	1,277
87.20	24,786	5,049	20.4	2,002	39.7	3,047
88.10	25,505	1,665	6.5	631	37.9	1,034
88.20	34,454	3,674	10.7	1,298	35.3	2,376
89	7,578	493	6.5	180	36.5	313
90	36,828	4,124	11.2	1,644	39.9	2,480
91	23,430	386	1.6	146	37.8	240
92	1,786	68	3.8	21	30.9	47

See map on pages 154-155.

Table I–C: NUMBER AND PROPORTION OF PERSONS OF ITALIAN PARENTAGE, BY HEALTH AREAS, BRONX, NEW YORK CITY, 1930
(First and second generations)

Health Area (1)	Total Population (2)	Total Italian 1st & 2nd Generation (3)	% Total Italians in Total Population (4)	Foreign Born or 1st Generation Italians (5)	% Foreign Born in Total Italian Population (6)	Native Born or 2nd Generation Italians (7)
Total	1,265,258	165,004	13.0	67,732	41.0	97,272
1	6,694	380	5.7	166	43.7	214
2	9,154	673	7.4	241	35.8	432
3	37,328	1,485	4.0	617	41.5	868
4.10	27,127	1,556	5.7	606	38.9	950
4.20	23,596	3,740	15.9	1,382	37.0	2,358
5.10	15,073	1,746	11.6	642	36.8	1,104
5.20	17,520	6,175	35.2	2,426	39.3	3,749
6.10	20,251	11,040	54.5	4,406	39.9	6,634
6.20	11,963	6,803	56.9	2,573	37.8	4,230
7	6,888	1,015	14.7	368	36.3	647
8.10	23,496	4,988	21.2	2,070	41.5	2,918
8.20	8,058	3,734	46.3	1,526	40.9	2,208
9	32,708	1,706	5.2	688	40.3	1,018
10	25,709	8,525	33.2	3,792	44.5	4,733
11	25,058	20,212	80.7	8,860	43.8	11,352
12	32,317	9,770	30.2	4,195	42.9	5,575
13.10	15,223	2,926	19.2	897	30.7	2,029
13.20	11,757	2,875	24.5	1,100	38.3	1,775
14.10	2,712	864	31.9	352	40.7	512
14.20	19,508	5,130	26.3	2,082	40.6	3,048
15	37,616	969	2.6	379	39.1	590
16	28,681	1,033	3.6	408	39.5	625
17	21,202	3,657	17.2	1,537	42.0	2,120
18	18,964	2,094	11.0	861	41.1	1,233
19	28,886	4,843	16.8	2,106	43.5	2,737
20	30,732	1,133	3.7	464	41.0	669
21	41,629	1,408	3.4	603	42.8	805
22.10	26,818	488	1.8	180	36.9	308
22.20	30,973	1,012	3.3	400	39.5	612
23	40,136	697	1.7	287	41.2	410
24	21,559	1,357	6.3	569	41.9	788
25	29,875	910	3.0	354	38.9	556
26	24,272	1,721	7.1	675	39.2	1,046
27	27,429	854	3.1	340	39.8	514
28	19,621	1,569	8.0	658	41.9	911
29	32,042	1,082	3.4	470	43.4	612
30.10	22,677	2,217	9.8	903	40.7	1,314
30.20	21,363	2,417	11.3	949	39.3	1,468
30.30	7,304	1,090	14.9	379	34.8	711
31	14,695	1,952	13.3	754	38.6	1,198
32.10	12,471	2,721	21.8	992	36.5	1,729
32.20	5,719	692	12.1	177	25.6	515
33.10	19,737	757	3.8	293	38.7	464
33.20	30,144	1,464	4.9	586	40.0	878
34	16,577	1,225	7.4	477	38.9	748
35	26,862	1,362	5.1	560	41.1	802
36	22,183	792	3.6	363	45.8	429
37	24,987	593	2.4	269	45.4	324
38	16,147	7,968	49.3	3,369	42.3	4,599
39	19,332	6,431	33.3	2,793	43.4	3,638
40	24,135	1,884	7.8	813	43.2	1,071
41	22,396	2,576	11.5	1,117	43.4	1,459
42	24,199	1,459	6.0	614	42.1	845
43	15,527	739	4.8	310	41.9	428
44	23,649	1,887	8.0	797	42.2	1,090
45	19,161	1,198	6.3	515	43.0	683
46	18,560	1,538	8.3	654	42.5	884
47	23,939	1,772	7.4	702	39.6	1,070
48	1,303	101	7.8	66	65.3	35

(SEE MAP ON PAGE 14)

See map on pages 156-157.

Table I—D: NUMBER AND PROPORTION OF PERSONS OF ITALIAN PARENTAGE, BY HEALTH AREAS, QUEENS, NEW YORK CITY, 1930
(First and second generations)

Health Area (1)	Total Population (2)	Total Italian 1st & 2nd Generation (3)	% Total Italians in Total Population (4)	Foreign Born or 1st Generation Italians (5)	% Foreign Born In Total Italian Generation Population (6)	Native Born or 2nd Generation Italians (7)
Total	1,079,129	127,381	11.8	50,307	39.5	77,074
1.10	23,018	5,043	21.9	2,357	46.7	2,686
1.20	20,909	2,466	11.8	1,010	41.0	1,456
2	24,450	1,315	5.4	517	39.3	798
3	26,672	8,321	31.2	3,579	43.0	4,742
4	33,835	4,402	13.0	1,812	41.2	2,590
5	31,575	2,673	8.5	978	36.6	1,695
6.10	17,759	5,242	29.5	2,162	41.2	3,080
6.20	11,209	1,544	13.8	638	41.3	906
7	28,917	12,371	42.8	4,988	40.3	7,383
8	11,519	786	6.8	320	40.7	466
9	32,816	2,124	6.5	825	38.8	1,299
10.10	21,058	862	4.1	371	43.0	491
10.20	24,428	2,505	10.3	1,117	44.6	1,388
11	28,699	10,772	37.5	4,790	44.5	5,982
12	19,687	2,715	13.8	1,097	40.4	1,618
13.10	16,836	645	3.8	230	35.7	415
13.20	15,209	943	6.2	376	39.9	567
14.10	8,229	768	9.3	289	37.6	479
14.20	17,220	1,052	6.1	400	38.0	652
15	17,344	11,426	65.9	4,283	37.5	7,143
16	18,743	939	5.0	338	36.0	601
17	29,727	2,046	6.9	680	33.2	1,366
18.10	18,204	1,026	5.6	392	38.2	634
18.20	18,787	1,601	8.5	567	35.4	1,034
19	26,046	1,208	4.6	438	36.3	770
20	10,619	1,485	14.0	471	31.7	1,014
21.10	16,479	969	5.9	363	37.5	606
21.20	18,834	865	4.6	408	47.2	457
22	22,292	873	3.9	322	36.9	551
23	24,313	980	4.0	386	39.4	594
24	26,706	981	3.7	343	35.0	638
25	26,151	1,065	4.1	380	35.7	685
26	25,942	1,178	4.5	454	38.5	724
27	28,332	1,720	6.1	675	39.2	1,045
28.10	16,113	539	3.3	175	32.5	364
28.20	15,272	594	3.9	204	34.3	390
29	27,871	847	3.0	298	35.2	549
30	30,963	7,062	22.8	2,612	37.0	4,450
31	31,001	3,679	11.9	1,405	38.2	2,274
32	33,410	2,942	8.8	1,006	34.2	1,936
33	22,688	3,498	15.4	1,342	38.4	2,156
34	25,746	3,772	14.7	1,439	38.1	2,333
35.10	14,964	1,526	10.2	620	40.6	906
35.20	19,648	715	3.6	245	34.3	470
35.30	25,727	1,153	4.5	400	34.7	753
36.10	28,074	3,142	11.2	1,120	35.6	2,022
36.20	8,040	710	8.8	280	39.4	430
37	16,315	1,092	6.7	372	34.1	720
38	18,621	1,126	6.0	414	36.8	712
39	2,112	73	3.5	19	26.0	54

(SEE MAP ON OPPOSITE PAGE)

See map on pages 158-159.

Table I—E: NUMBER AND PROPORTION OF PERSONS OF ITALIAN PARENTAGE, BY HEALTH AREAS, RICHMOND, NEW YORK CITY, 1930
(First and Second Generations)

Health Area (1)	Total Population (2)	Total Italian 1st & 2nd Generation (3)	% Total Italians in Total Population (4)	Foreign Born or 1st Generation Italians (5)	% Foreign Born in Total Italian Population (6)	Native Born or 2nd Generation Italians (7)
Total	158,346	29,935	18.9	11,036	36.9	18,899
1	10,754	2,148	20.0	836	38.9	1,312
2	19,731	4,221	21.4	1,528	36.2	2,693
3	19,172	3,571	18.6	1,350	37.8	2,221
4	23,817	4,535	19.0	1,654	36.5	2,881
5	14,712	1,541	10.5	545	35.4	996
6	16,192	1,912	11.8	815	42.6	1,097
7	12,639	4,481	35.5	1,477	33.0	3,004
8	15,987	1,045	6.5	264	25.3	781
9	21,784	6,323	29.0	2,520	39.9	3,803
10	3,558	147	4.1	47	32.0	100

See map on pages 160-161.

Table I—F:

DISTRIBUTION OF ITALIAN POPULATION, FIRST AND SECOND GENERATIONS, AND THEIR PROPORTIONS TO TOTAL POPULATION, AND TO POPULATION OF FOREIGN STOCK, BY BOROUGHS, NEW YORK CITY, 1930

Borough (1)	Total Population (2)	Total Italian 1st & 2nd Generation (3)	% Total Italians in Total Population (4)	Foreign Born or 1st Generation Italian (5)	% Foreign Born in Total Italian Population (6)
Totals	6,930,446	1,070,355	15.44	440,250	41.1
Manhattan	1,867,312	260,702	13.96	117,740	45.2
Brooklyn	2,560,401	487,344	19.03	193,435	39.7
Bronx	1,265,258	165,004	13.04	67,732	41.0
Queens	1,079,129	127,381	11.80	50,307	39.5
Richmond	158,346	29,924	18.90	11,036	36.9

Borough (1)	Native Born or 2nd Generation Italian (7)	Total Foreign Stock (8)	Total Foreign Born White (9)	Total Native White of Foreign or Mixed Parentage (10)	% Total Italians in total Foreign Stock (11)
Totals	630,105	5,082,025	2,293,400	2,788,625	21.1
Manhattan	142,962	1,250,492	641,618	608,874	20.8
Brooklyn	293,909	1,995,723	868,770	1,126,953	24.4
Bronx	97,272	1,038,323	477,342	560,981	15.9
Queens	77,074	693,890	266,150	427,740	18.4
Richmond	18,888	103,597	39,520	64,077	28.9

REPRINT from "ATLANTICA", September, 1934

*Copyright 1934, Casa Italiana Educational Bureau

Table II. NATIVITY COMPOSITION FOR SELECTED ITALIAN HEALTH AREAS, NEW YORK CITY, 1930
(in per cents)

Health Area	Native White Native Parents	Native White Foreign Parents	Foreign Born White	Negro and Others	Total
Manhattan No. 21	7.7	53.0	38.1	1.2	100.
Manhattan No. 22	6.7	53.6	38.2	1.5	100.
Brooklyn No. 82	7.4	52.7	39.2	.7	100.
Bronx No. 11	3.2	52.8	43.6	.4	100.

Table III. PERCENTAGE DISTRIBUTION BY AGE AND NATIVITY FOR SELECTED ITALIAN HEALTH AREAS, NEW YORK CITY, 1930

	0-5 years	5-14 years	15-24 years	25-34 years	35-44 years	45-64 years	65 & over	Age Unknown	Total
MANHATTAN HEALTH AREA 21									
Foreign Born White	.6	2.9	8.3	22.2	26.7	31.8	7.5	.0	100.
Native White									
Foreign or Mixed Parentage	16.2	39.5	29.4	10.0	3.5	1.2	.2	.0	100.
Native White of Native Parentage	32.9	31.0	13.9	10.8	5.9	4.8	.7	.0	100.
MANHATTAN HEALTH AREA 22									
Foreign Born White	.3	2.8	7.3	19.9	29.5	32.5	7.6	.1	100.
Native White									
Foreign or Mixed Parentage	15.4	39.1	30.0	10.3	3.5	1.4	.2	.1	100.
Native White of Native Parentage	36.0	39.7	12.2	6.2	2.7	2.9	.3	.0	100.
BROOKLYN HEALTH AREA 82									
Foreign Born White	.1	2.2	8.9	23.4	27.8	31.3	6.3	.0	100.
Native White									
Foreign or Mixed Parentage	14.6	38.6	29.8	11.5	3.3	1.8	.3	.1	100.
Native White of Native Parentage	27.3	27.8	15.4	14.5	7.1	6.0	1.7	.2	100.
BRONX HEALTH AREA 11									
Foreign Born White	.3	2.5	8.2	24.7	31.1	26.8	6.4	.0	100.
Native White									
Foreign or Mixed Parentage	18.2	41.3	28.6	8.3	2.1	1.0	.5	.0	100.
Native White of Native Parentage	35.1	31.1	13.7	9.3	6.1	2.9	1.5	.3	100.

Table IV. PERCENTAGE DISTRIBUTION OF THE POPULATION OF SELECTED HEALTH AREAS UNDER AND OVER 21 YEARS OF AGE, NEW YORK CITY, 1930

(Health Areas selected as predominantly Italian, Jewish, Irish or German)

Health Area	Per Cent Under 21	Per Cent Over 21	Nationality	Health Area	Per Cent Under 21	Per Cent Over 21	Nationality
21	49.3	50.7	Italian	3	26.8	73.2	Jewish
22	48.5	51.5	"	6	23.8	76.2	"
26	49.2	50.8	"	9	25.5	74.5	"
68	38.1	61.9	"	34	17.6	82.4	"
69	46.3	53.7	"	71	39.3	60.7	"
78	42.7	57.3	"	72	40.3	59.7	"
				75	42.4	57.6	"
				80	42.6	57.4	"
14	24.6	75.4	Irish	37	27.9	72.0	German
45	39.0	61.0	"	38	32.8	67.2	"
51	30.7	69.3	"				
61	20.7	79.3	"				

Table V. COMPARISON OF THE AGE DISTRIBUTION OF SELECTED HEALTH AREAS WITH THE TOTAL POPULATION OF THE RESPECTIVE BOROUGHS, NEW YORK CITY, 1930

(Distributions in per cents of Total Population of the Respective Areas)

SELECTED HEALTH AREAS and ENTIRE BOROUGHS	Under 5 yrs.	5-14 yrs.	15-24 yrs.	25-34 yrs.	35-44 yrs.	45-64 yrs.	65 yrs. & over	Age Unknown	Total
Manhattan Health Areas 21 and 22	10.8	24.7	20.0	14.5	13.4	13.5	3.1	—	100.
Borough of Manhattan	6.1	13.8	17.7	20.6	18.1	19.3	4.2	.2	100.
Brooklyn Health Area 82	10.3	21.4	21.4	16.8	13.4	13.8	2.8	.1	100.
Borough of Brooklyn	8.4	18.1	19.7	18.4	15.1	16.6	3.7	—	100.
Bronx Health Area 11	10.9	23.9	19.1	15.5	14.9	12.3	3.1	.3	100.
Borough of Bronx	8.2	17.0	19.0	19.9	16.4	16.0	3.4	.1	100.

143

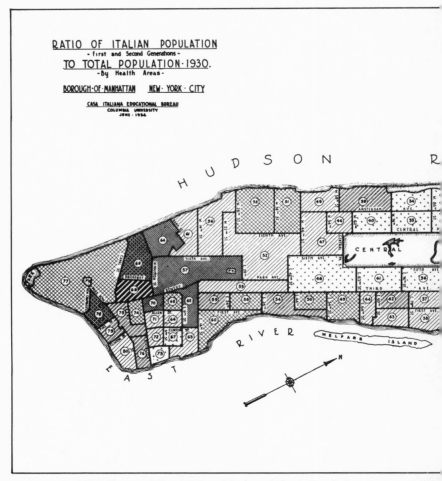

NOTE: The areas 2.10 and 2.20 are interchanged; the shadings in these two areas should

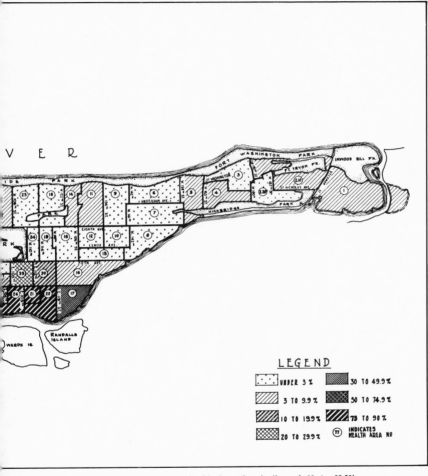

LEGEND

UNDER 3 %   30 TO 49.9 %

3 TO 9.9 %   50 TO 74.9 %

10 TO 19.9 %   75 TO 90 %

20 TO 29.9 %   ⑰ INDICATES
                   HEALTH AREA Nº

transposed accordingly. HEALTH AREA 59 should show the shading of 20 to 29.9%.

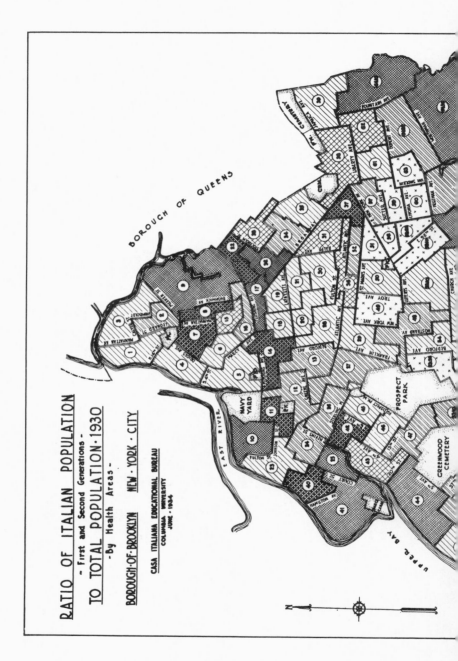

RATIO OF ITALIAN POPULATION
- First and Second Generations -
TO TOTAL POPULATION · 1930
- By Health Areas -

BOROUGH-OF-BROOKLYN   NEW · YORK · CITY

CASA ITALIANA EDUCATIONAL BUREAU
COLUMBIA UNIVERSITY
JUNE · 1934

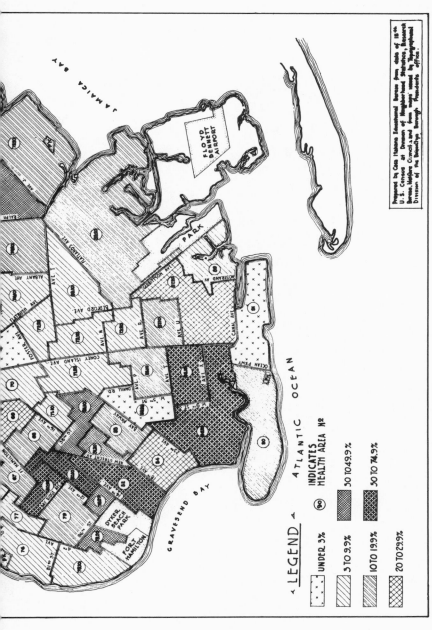

Health Area 85.20 should be shaded to show from 20 to 29.9%.

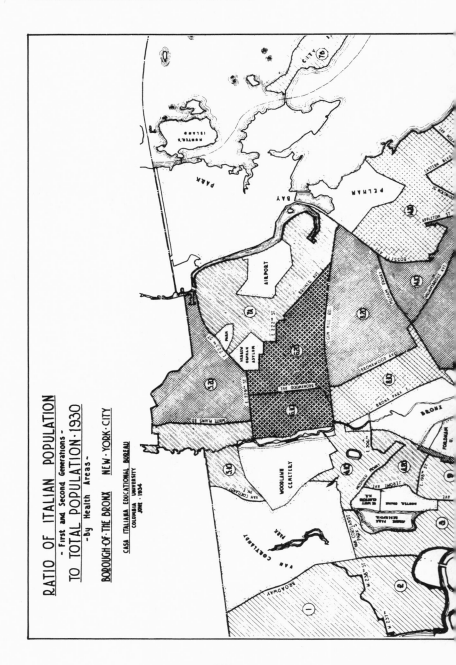

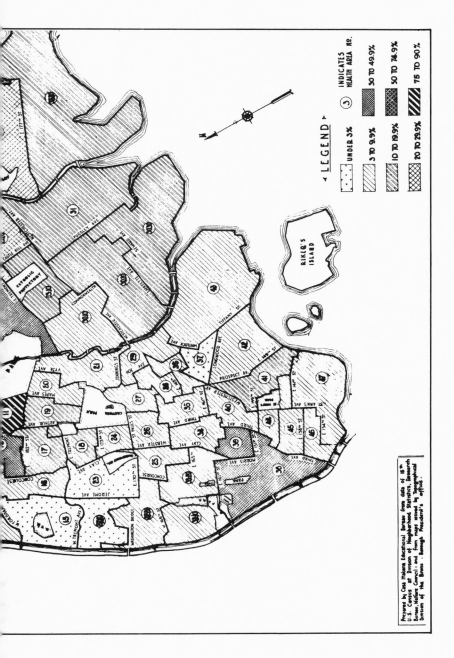

Prepared by Casa Italiana Educational Bureau from data of 15th U.S. Census at Division of Neighborhood Statistics, Research Bureau, Welfare Council: and from maps issued by Topographical Division of the Bronx - Borough President's office.

‹ LEGEND ›

UNDER 3%

3 TO 9.9%

10 TO 19.9%

20 TO 29.9%

③ INDICATES HEALTH AREA №.

30 TO 49.9%

50 TO 74.9%

75 TO 90%

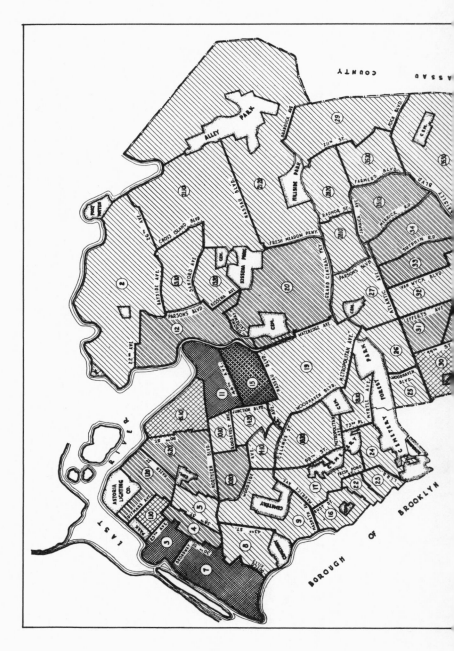

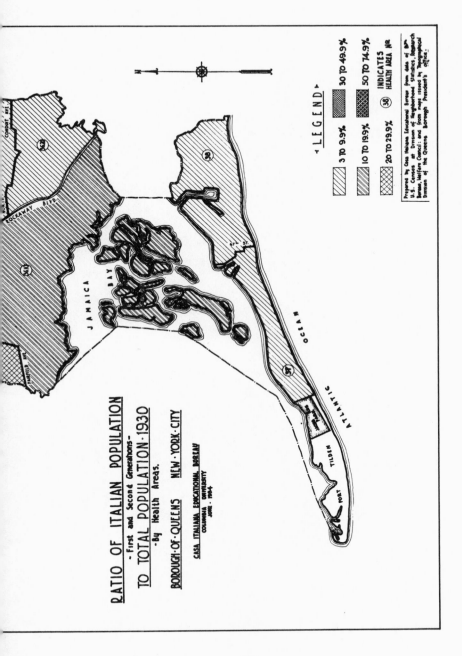

RATIO OF ITALIAN POPULATION
- First and Second Generations -
TO TOTAL POPULATION · 1930
- By Health Areas.

BOROUGH·OF·QUEENS   NEW·YORK·CITY

CASA ITALIANA EDUCATIONAL BUREAU
COLUMBIA UNIVERSITY
JUNE · 1954

· L E G E N D ·

3 TO 9.9%
10 TO 19.9%
20 TO 29.9%
30 TO 49.9%
50 TO 74.9%
30   INDICATES
HEALTH AREA Nº

Prepared by Casa Italiana Educational Bureau from data of
U.S. Census at Division of Neighborhood Statistics, Research
Bureau, Welfare Council; and from maps issued by Topographical
Division of the Queens Borough President's office.

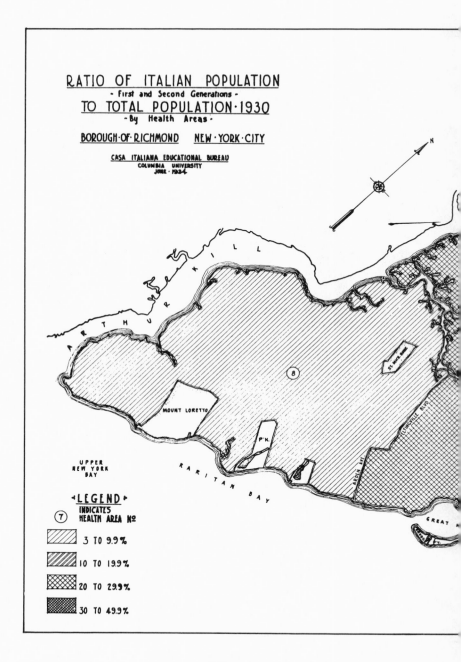

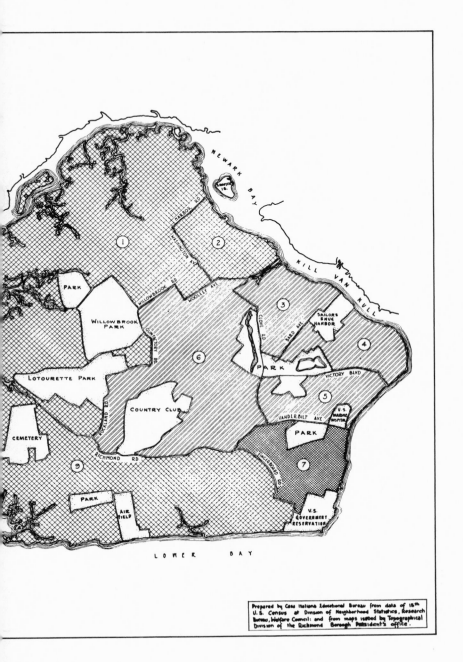

Prepared by Casa Italiana Educational Bureau from data of 15th U.S. Census at Division of Neighborhood Statistics, Research Bureau, Welfare Council; and from maps issued by Topographical Division of the Richmond Borough President's office.

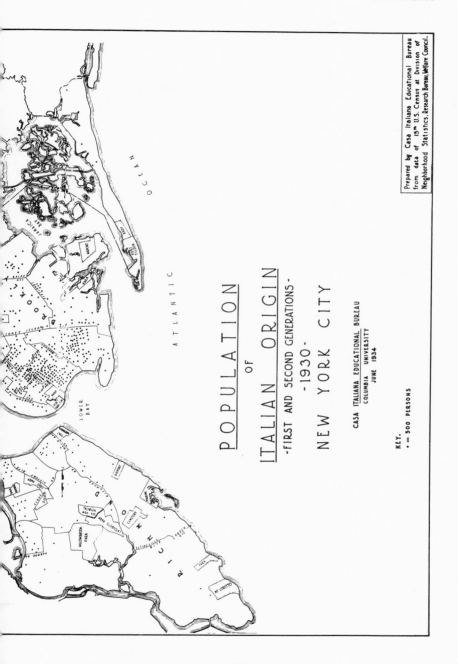

POPULATION

OF

ITALIAN ORIGIN

-FIRST AND SECOND GENERATIONS-

-1930-

NEW YORK CITY

CASA ITALIANA EDUCATIONAL BUREAU
COLUMBIA UNIVERSITY
JUNE 1934

KEY.
• = 500 PERSONS

Prepared by Casa Italiana Educational Bureau from data of 15ᵗʰ U.S. Census at Division of Neighborhood Statistics, Research Bureau, Welfare Council.

OCCUPATIONAL TRENDS
OF ITALIANS
IN NEW YORK CITY

BY

JOHN J. D'ALESANDRE

●

BULLETIN No. 8.
CASA ITALIANA EDUCATIONAL BUREAU
COLUMBIA UNIVERSITY, NEW YORK CITY

FOREWORD

The most pressing need of the new immigrant who came to the shores of America was to solve his economic problem. The job (which became "la giobba" amongst the Italian immigrants to our shores) was the immediate concern of the newly arrived. Any job! Anywhere! The occupational skills the immigrant had acquired, often by years of training in his own coutry, usually found no outlet in the new country. The worker had little or no occupational choice. Long hours, low wages, hard labor, tedious, nerve-racking work,—in short, exploitation—were his portion. The entire structure of our American industrial life rested heavily upon the backs of these immigrant workers.

Of these workers, the Italian immigrant was the most recent who came to America to make a living for himself and for his family. As in the case of the immigrant of the older racial groups, no provision was made to utilize his abilities or his training. As soon as he landed he was swallowed up in the tremendous whirlpool of our American industrial life. With careful planning, much might have been done for these workers and their children. Much might have been avoided—particularly those situations which are now having such deleterious repercussions in many of the slum areas of our large cities. The insecurity of the worker, the shifting, unstable social conditions produced these situations.

The Casa Italiana Educational Bureau was organized as a fact-finding institution which, in cooperation with other agencies, would study social and economic factors dealing with the Italian population in New York City and in the other parts of our country. This study is in line with the aim of the Bureau. It is hoped that the occupational trends of Italians shown herein will prove of some value. Further studies in this field will soon be available. To conclude: this study centers its attention upon the first-generation Italians. What of the second-generation Italians? The American-born child of Italian immigrant parents? Has he any direction? If so, in what direction is he going? These and many related problems should be the direct concern of all our educational institutions. Guidance, vocational, and educational—is receiving the increased attention of our federal, state, and city educational authorities. Earning a living, and living are intimately interwoven. The school must educate for both.

LEONARD COVELLO
Executive Director,
Casa Italiana Educational Bureau

OCCUPATIONAL TRENDS OF ITALIANS IN NEW YORK CITY

JOHN J. D'ALESANDRE

Research Associate, Casa Italiana Educational Bureau

ACKNOWLEDGEMENTS

The author wishes to make the following acknowledgements:

To Miss Elizabeth Roby for her aid and suggestions.

To the Division of Vital Statistics, Department of Health, New York City, for making available the records used in this study.

To the Works Division of the Emergency Relief Bureau, New York City, for providing a staff of competent workers, which makes the work of the Casa Italiana Educational Bureau possible.

JOHN J. D'ALESANDRE

INTRODUCTION

Those of us who have been working with and among Italian groups, whether it be with the first or second-generation Italians, or both, in order to better understand the problems of their adjustment, have often felt a need for information concerning occupational activities of Italians in the United States. The material herein is presented for the value it may possess to the many teachers interested in knowing the occupational distribution and trends that affect the children of Italian parents. Many leading educators feel that it is important to have a more comprehensive vocational guidance program for the children in our schools, which should be incorporated into our school curriculum. It is generally recognized that this would to a great extent act as a corrective to many problems which the schools are at present unable to cope with. The occupational analysis of this group may be of value to those who are trying to devise a vocational or educational guidance plan for a group. It may be of value also to social workers or

159

personnel workers who are giving advice concerning a choice of occupation.

An analysis of vocational choices made by high school boys of Italian origin in an unpublished study by the Casa Italiana Educational Bureau, shows that the choice is often unintelligent, and in many cases is not directed; nor has it any continuity toward a definite aim in life. This has been shown to be frequently true in many studies of occupational activities. Whereas, in the United States there are actually several thousand occupational activities, these boys mentioned less than two hundred. Furthermore, their choice was not well distributed even among the two hundred lines of work. To further emphasize the limited distribution of choice, the choice of the boys was concentrated in about ten leading occupations. There was a marked preponderance of a choice for the professions. Of course, it is to be expected that a high school group would seek a higher level in occupations.

The discrepancies between the choice of vocations and the status of workers now employed can be traced to many causes. Youth is always hopeful and optimistic, and inclined to look forward to great things. Most children are ignorant of the conditions existing in the occupational world. They have little or no conception of the many types of work, or of the qualifications needed by the worker for the work. Youth is influenced by the prevalent social attitude which glorifies certain kinds of work as "white collar" vocations and deprecates the more "menial" occupations. On the other hand there is the sad fact to be reckoned with that the choice of occupation is often determined by stern necessity and the need to accept whatever employment may be offered, whether or not it may be suitable or according to the interests of the boy.

When dealing with young people as part of a guidance program, it is valuable to know the occupation of the parent, since it may affect the future of the child in one or more of the following ways:

1. The occupation of the parent generally determines his earning power and often the economic status of the family. Obviously, this exerts a direct influence upon the boy's chances for a prolonged schooling.

2. The father may try to influence his son to follow his own line of work.

3. As more frequently happens, the father may react against his own occupation, and may try to have his son trained along some line which is entirely different.

4. In these days of scarcity of employment opportunities, we must know of any possibility of employment for a boy, and whether or not the father can give him help in finding his first job.

5. If we know the father's occupation, it gives us one more clue concerning the environment in which the boy is growing up.

6. If the occupational background of the parent is limited along certain lines, it may suggest what occupational information or misinformation the boy may have received, and hence what type of information is most needed from us.

PURPOSE OF THE SURVEY

This first and partial analysis of some of the material gathered by the Casa Italiana Educational Bureau was made with the hope that it might prove to be of value to those who have indicated a need for and an interest in occupational information concerning the Italian in New York City. We hope to arouse a recognition for the need of a body of facts that can be further developed, studied, compared, and analyzed by those who are interested in our Italian population and its many problems of adjustment in a modern complex urban civilization. This is an initial attempt. There are many lists, compilations, charts, and tables that are still available for more complete study and analysis of the occupational problem. The main purpose of this study shall have been achieved if it will have stimulated in the student of social and economic life of the Italian in our coutry an interest in the social and economic implications which more comprehensive data might reveal.

TECHNIQUES

It is of the utmost importance in a project of this sort that the material be scientifically and uniformly gathered, compiled, and analyzed and that the resultant material need as little explanation and weighing as possible to make comparison valid. We have attempted to fill these requirements. We hope that the method and technique used in presenting and analyzing the following material has been reduced to such form as to make it of interest and value to the general public.

The matter of the classification of occupations is a very difficult one to handle. There is no satisfactory and generally accepted classification. For this reason we have made no attempt to group the occupations studied, except in the cases of the professions and clerical occupations. The Millbank Foundation Classification of 1900, the Census Classification, the Counts Social Status Scale, the Barr Scale of

TABLE VII.—PERCENT DISTRIBUTION OF ITALIANS IN PROFESSIONAL AND CLERICAL OCCUPATIONS FROM BIRTH, MARRIAGES AND DEATH RECORDS, NEW YORK CITY, 1916 AND 1931

	Births				Deaths				Marriages			
	1916		1931		1916		1931		1916		1931	
	No	%	No	%	No	%	No	%	No	%	No	%
Professional	380	1.2	266	1.6	34	1.4	64	1.7	108	1.5	80	2.1
Clerical	224	.7	327	1.9	44	1.8	81	2.1	149	2.0	155	4.1

Occupational Intelligence, Menger's Social Status Scale, the data compiled from Army Mental Tests or any other material do not permit of comparative analysis or study because of the different methods and techniques used in obtaining and classifying occupations. Largely because of the variety of these classifications we were in this study unable to make any analysis, comparable with the afore-mentioned studies.

SCOPE OF DATA

The data were selected because they were the only available information on occupations offering so large a sampling of the Italian population in New York City.

The statistical compilation was made from the total number of birth, marriage, and death certificates of New York City residents for the years 1916 and 1931 as contained in the original records of the Department of Health for the City of New York. The occupations from the birth certificates were those of the father if either or both parents were born in Italy. The marriage records used were cases where either the bride or groom or both were born in Italy. The occupation was of the groom. The death records used were of the males of either Italian birth or Italian parentage. The occupation of the deceased as recorded on the death certificate was taken for this study.

LIMITATION OF THE STUDY DUE TO THESE CONDITIONS

Cognizance is taken of the fact that the study contains many conditions that have not as yet been investigated and evaluated. The birth and marriage records, obviously, do not include the unmarried males who are engaged in occupations. The age-group distribution of the 1916 groupings as compared to 1931 groupings, because of the immigration problem explained herein, would tend to make the 1931 grouping older and may be a factor in explaining some of the changes in the occupational ranks, numbers, and percentages. The immigrants who make up the 1916 group contain an older age-group distribution than a cross section of a population group with a normal percentage of infants, children, and youths.

While it is true, for example, that a person may have been married in New York City in 1916 and 1931; or given birth to children both in 1916 and 1931, this possibility of duplication in listing of the recorded occupations on birth and marriage record is negligible.

Another factor to be considered is that changes have occurred within industry during these fifteen years. Regardless of nationality grouping, a knowledge of such change is very important and a study is necessary of the total situation to make a thorough and valid analysis of occupational trends in New York City.

The death records were filled out and sent to the Board of Health by doctors and undertakers. The recording of births was dependent upon the filling in of the information by doctors and midwives. In the marriage records the personal factor might enter more than on the other records. The prospective groom in stating his occupation might try to raise his occupational status. Moreover, the occupation as recorded in all these records does not mention the industry.

Due to the method of recording, it has been difficult to classify these occupations into skilled, semi-skilled and unskilled. Undoubtedly many among the unskilled may have changed the nomenclature of their particular work. There is less likelihood of a change of occupation and of nomenclature in the recorded listings of skilled and professional occupations. All these factors affect the accuracy of these records.

In presenting the following tables, I to VI inclusive, the following steps were taken:—The transcribed birth, marriage, and death records were each arranged in alphabetical order, according to name of occupation. The numbers in each occupation were then totalled and listed. Because the birth records of 1916 numbering 31,556 were the largest group, the occupations containing 100 or more cases in that series were selected as the basis of comparison for all six series. Since the number of occupations here was 36, we have included the first 36 occupations for all the tables even though they represent less than 100 cases.

TABLES I AND II

In reading Tables I and II, it will be seen that "Laborer," the largest grouping for both years, formed 50.4 per cent in 1916 and 31.4 per cent in 1931 of the total cases in these respective series. This may be interpreted to mean that our immigration laws had a decided effect on this grouping. In 1917 the act to restrict illiterate immigrants was passed. The Emergency Quota Act of 1921 limited the number of immigrants to three per cent of the number of each nationality living in the United States in 1910. This, however, was not quite as effective in reducing Italian immigration as the Johnson Act of 1924 which changed the percentage from three to two and changed the basis on which the number was calculated from the 1910 census to the 1890 census, and provided for further restriction after 1927. The economic depression in our industries, especially building and construction, since 1929 and the advance in the mechanization of our industries, (e. g. steam shovels, automatic machinery, etc.) may have lessened the demand for laborers causing them to go into other types of employment. This may explain the decrease of nineteen per cent in the number of laborers.

"Shoemaker" retained the rank of fourth position, but the percentages were 2.9 and 3.7 for 1916 and 1931 respectively. The difficulty of nomenclature applies throughout this study. For example, there were listed Cobbler, Heel Maker, Shoe Maker, etc. However, because it seemed to us that any arbitrary grouping or combining would be largely subjective, we adhered to the name of occupation as given. The status of the unionized factory "shoe worker" and the "cobbler" who maintains a small shop would be different in their economic, social, and occupational levels.

"Carpenter" dropped from fifth to sixth in its rank among occupations, but increased from 2.1 per cent in 1916 to 2.5 per cent for 1931. It would be significant to carry on a further study of these differences and the causes of them in view of the fact that building for 1931 materially decreased and there was a decrease in the use of wood in the building industry in New York City. It may mean that some of the unskilled workers of 1916 have entered the skilled field of carpentry.

"Driver" showed a change in rank from seventh to eighteenth but the change in percentage was not so great. Here again we encountered a number of various classifications that might have been included in "Driver," e. g. Milk Wagon Driver, Teamster, Truckman, and Chauffeur.

TABLE VIII—PROPORTION OF ITALIAN BIRTHS, MARRIAGES, AND DEATHS TO TOTALS RECORDED IN NEW YORK CITY, 1916 AND 1931

	Italian	Total	Percentage of Italian to Total
Births—1916	31,556	137,664	22.9
Births—1931	16,945	115,621	14.7
Deaths—1916	2,504	77,801	3.2
Deaths—1931	3,778	77,418	4.9
Marriages—1916	7,341	54,782	13.4
Marriages—1931	3,785	61,574	6.1

"Longshoreman" showed a change of from sixth to eleventh in ranking. The difference in percentage was slight. The percentage for 1916 was 1.9 and for 1931, 1.5. Most of the longshoremen are unionized and their remuneration is fairly high. There are among them those skilled or experienced in proper handling, storing, tying slings, fastening nets, and the use of the winches.

"Coal man" changed in ranking from eighth to one hundred seventy-second. There were 325 or 1.0 per cent for 1916 and 4 or 0.2 per cent for 1931. The decrease in the use of the coal stoves probably accounts for most of this change.

"Business Man" ranked ninth in 1916 and twenty-third in 1931. There were 289 (.9 per cent) in 1916 and 130 (.8 per cent) in 1931. "Business Man" is a classification which may include anyone from a proprietor of a small one-man business to the head of a large organization. The various "dealers" may or may not be classified as business men.

"Mechanic" held its ranking fairly well. There were 289 for 1916 and 383 for 1931. Their percentages vary greatly in that they were .9 per cent and 2.1 per cent respectively. "Mechanic" may include a wide range of skilled occupations as Electrician, Machinist, Maintenance Man, and others.

"Street Cleaner" ranked twenty-sixth in 1916 and seventieth in 1931. There were 143 (.4 per cent) in 1916 and 22 (.1 per cent) in 1931.

"Piano Maker" showed a great decrease in rank, number, and percentage. It would be interesting to determine all the factors influencing these changes. The development of the Victrola, and later the radio, was an important factor.

The decrease of "Bartender" may be attributed to the prohibition laws.

TABLE I — LEADING OCCUPATIONS: ITALIAN FATHERS OF CHILDREN BORN IN NEW YORK CITY IN 1916†

Rank	Occupation	Number	Per cent	Rank in Table II
	Total	31,556	100.0	
	36 *Leading Occupations*	27,209	86.2	
1	Laborer	15,905	50.4	(1)
2	Tailor	1,697	5.4	(3)
3	Barber	1,667	5.3	(2)
4	Shoemaker	909	2.9	(4)
5	Carpenter	651	2.1	(6)
6	Longshoreman	596	1.9	(11)
7	Driver	546	1.7	(18)
8	Coal Man	325	1.0	(172)
9	Business Man	289	.9	(23)
10	Mechanic	278	.9	(9)
11	Cook	258	.8	(22)
12	Baker	257	.8	(14)
13	Painter	256	.8	(8)
14	Bricklayer	237	.8	(16)
15	Printer	214	.7	(25)
16	Fruit Dealer	199	.6	(20)
17	Plasterer	198	.6	(10)
18	Presser	195	.6	(19)
19	Bootblack	192	.6	(37)
20	Butcher	191	.6	(15)
21	Waiter	176	.6	(33)
22	Proprietor	167	.5	(32)
23	Musician	155	.5	(30)
24	Merchant	151	.5	(41)
25	Salesman	147	.5	(13)
26	Street Cleaner	143	.5	(70)
27	Machinist	140	.4	(29)
28	Mason	137	.4	(34)
29	Piano Maker	131	.4	(261)
30	Clerk	130	.4	(12)
31	Operator	125	.4	(129)
32	Grocer	118	.4	(39)
33	Bartender	112	.4	(287)
34	Porter	108	.3	(44)
35	Ice Man	106	.3	(17)
36	Chauffeur	103	.3	(5)

All other occupations	4,092	13.0	
Unknown	255	.8	

†*The source of the data in this table is the birth certificates on file at the Division of Vital Statistics, Department of Health, New York City.*

TABLE II — LEADING OCCUPATIONS: ITALIAN FATHERS OF CHILDREN BORN IN NEW YORK CITY IN 1931

Rank	Occupation	Number	Per cent	Rank in Table I
	Total	16,945	100.0	
	36 *Leading Occupations*	13,700	80.5	
1	Laborer	5,321	31.4	(1)
2	Barber	850	5.0	(3)
3	Tailor	713	4.2	(2)
4	Shoemaker	633	3.7	(4)
5	Chauffeur	608	3.6	(36)
6	Carpenter	429	2.5	(5)
7	Ice Dealer	392	2.3	*
8	Painter	379	2.2	(13)
9	Mechanic	363	2.1	(10)
10	Plasterer	306	1.8	(17)
11	Longshoreman	257	1.5	(6)
12	Clerk	253	1.5	(30)
13	Salesman	250	1.5	(25)
14	Baker	231	1.4	(12)
15	Butcher	228	1.3	(20)
16	Bricklayer	216	1.3	(14)
17	Ice Man	192	1.1	(35)
18	Driver	180	1.1	(7)
19	Presser	170	1.0	(18)
20	Fruit Dealer	142	.8	(16)
21	Ice and Coal	139	.8	*
22	Cook	133	.8	(11)
23	Business Man	130	.8	(9)
24	Peddler	116	.7	*
25	Printer	114	.7	(15)
26	Trucking	101	.6	*
27	Plumber	99	.6	*
28	Electrician	93	.5	*
29	Machinist	93	.5	(27)
30	Musician	89	.5	(23)
31	Contractor	88	.5	*
32	Proprietor	88	.5	(22)
33	Waiter	87	.5	(21)
34	Mason	76	.4	(28)
35	Foreman	73	.4	*
36	Cabinet Maker	69	.4	*

All other occupations	3,053	18.4	
Unknown	117	.7	
Unemployed	75	.4	

* *Does not appear in leading occupations Table 1.*

TABLE II (*Continued*)

Leading occupations in 1916 (Table 1), which do not appear in Leading Occupations for 1931 (Table II)

Rank in 1931	Occupation	Number	Per cent	Rank in Table 1
37	Bootblack	68	.4	(19)
39	Grocer	59	.3	(32)
41	Merchant	56	.3	(24)
44	Porter	49	.3	(34)
70	Street Cleaner	22	.1	(26)
129	Operator	9	.1	(31)
172	Coal Man	4	—	(8)
261	Piano Maker	2	—	(29)
287	Bartender	1	—	(33)

†*The source of the data in this table is the birth certificates on file at the Division of Vital Statistics, Department of Health, New York City.*

TABLES III AND IV

Tables III and IV give the occupations of the grooms as gathered from the 7,341 New York City marriage records of 1916 and 3,785 New York City marriage records for 1931.

"Laborer" in the marriage records (See Tables III and IV) showed 32.5 per cent for 1916 and 10.6 per cent in 1931.

"Tailor" changed in ranking from second with 6.8 per cent in 1916 to fourth with 3.7 per cent in 1931.

"Barber" in the marriage series again as in the birth series maintained a fairly constant rank and percentage.

"Shoemaker" dropped in rank from fourth in 1916 to fifth in 1931, with the percentage changing from 3.5 to 2.9.

"Driver" as in the birth records again shows a great decrease in per cent and ranking. "Chauffeur" showed an opposite trend.

Notice particularly the variation in rank or percentages or both for the following occupations: Carpenter, Machinist, Fruit Dealer Longshoreman, Salesman, Plasterer, Musician, Cigar Maker, and Hatter.

The data concerning marriages in 1916 and births in 1916 may well be taken as typical of the parents of children now in our High Schools—ages 14 to 18. This data, therefore, should be particularly interesting to a vocational counselor at the present time.

TABLES V AND VI

Tables V and VI give the occupation of the deceased as recorded in the death certificates for 1916 and 1931, respectively. The listing of occupations was taken from those records

that gave Italy as the birthplace of the deceased, or of one, or both, of the deceased's parents.

The death records represent an older age group. The age-group distribution for 1931 show greater concentration toward the older ages than was shown in 1916.

The increase in the number of the "Retired" from 1916 to 1931 is to be expected in view of the above statement. They were only 2.4 per cent in 1916 and 7.1 per cent of the total group in 1931.

"Laborer" in Tables V and VI, again ranks number one, but did not show as great a difference in per cent as "Laborer" in the figures for births and marriages.

It may be surmised that the "Unknown" group variance is due to greater care and further instructions in filling out the death certificates in 1931.   * * *

The total number of cases in the birth records were 31,556. In listing the occupations for 1916, there were 580 different listed occupations given as the occupation at which the parent was employed. In listing the 1931 births there were 488 occupations reported for the 16,945 cases.

The occupations listed for the years 1916 and 1931, combined, showed 851 separate and differently-named occupations. These were obtained by listing alphabetically the occupations for 1916, then listing the occupations for 1931, combining these lists and eliminating all duplications. The 48,501 cases found in these two series thus list 851 different occupations.

In the marriage records of 1916, for a total number of 7,341 there were 403 separate occupations listed. For the year 1931 there were 481 occupations listed from the 3,785 cases The combined occupations listed for the years 1916 and 1931, showed a total of 664 occupations for the total of 11,127 cases.

In the death compilations for 1916, of the 2,504 cases, there were 243 occupations. In 3,778 cases for the year 1931, there were 295 occupations. For the years of 1916 and 1931 combined, there were listed 388 occupations from 6,282 death records.

As explained before, the writer made no attempt to combine or alter the occupations as actually written in the transcripts. It must be recognized, therefore, that with proper reporting this number would be somewhat reduced. For example, the listings of Auto Tester, Auto Mechanic, Auto Repairer, Auto Ignition Man, might reasonably have been included under one classification.

TABLE III — LEADING OCCUPATIONS: ITALIAN BRIDEGROOMS NEW YORK CITY, 1916

Rank	Occupation	Number	Per-cent	Rank in Table IV
	Total	7,341	100.0	
	36 Leading Occupations	5,671	77.4	
1	Laborer	2,389	32.5	(1)
2	Tailor	498	6.8	(4)
3	Barber	342	4.7	(3)
4	Shoemaker	255	3.5	(5)
5	Driver	200	2.7	(20)
6	Carpenter	152	2.1	(12)
7	Clerk	117	1.6	(6)
8	Machinist	115	1.6	(23)
9	Cook	104	1.4	(13)
10	Waiter	104	1.4	(17)
11	Presser	89	1.2	(14)
12	Coal Dealer	85	1.2	*
13	Painter	78	1.1	(7)
14	Chauffeur	76	1.0	(2)
15	Ice Dealer	73	1.0	(16)
16	Piano Maker	71	1.0	*
17	Mechanic	70	1.0	(8)
18	Fruit Dealer	68	.9	(29)
19	Butcher	66	.9	(15)
20	Longshoreman	64	.9	(63)
21	Salesman	64	.9	(9)
22	Baker	56	.8	(10)
23	Printer	55	.7	(18)
24	Bricklayer	50	.7	(19)
25	Mason	49	.7	(36)
26	Plasterer	48	.7	(11)
27	Musician	47	.6	(49)
28	Grocer	43	.6	(28)
29	Cigar Maker	39	.5	(69)
30	Operator	34	.5	(21)
31	Bootblack	33	.4	*
32	Merchant	33	.4	*
33	Electrican	27	.4	(25)
34	Hatter	27	.4	(72)
35	Cabinet Maker	25	.3	(26)
36	Candy Maker	25	.3	(40)
	All other occupations	1,315	17.8	
	Unknown	355	4.8	

* Does not appear in occupation reported by Italian bridegrooms in 1931.

TABLE IV — LEADING OCCUPATIONS: ITALIAN BRIDEGROOMS, NEW YORK CITY, 1931

Rank	Occupation	Number	Percent	Rank in Table III
	Total	3,785	100.0	
	36 Leading Occupations	2,495	66.3	
1	Laborer	402	10.6	(1)
2	Chauffeur	224	5.9	(14)
3	Barber	186	4.9	(3)
4	Tailor	140	3.7	(2)
5	Shoemaker	108	2.9	(4)
6	Clerk	105	2.8	(7)
7	Painter	99	2.6	(13)
8	Mechanic	94	2.5	(17)
9	Salesman	92	2.4	(21)
10	Baker	79	2.1	(22)
11	Plasterer	76	2.0	(26)
12	Carpenter	71	1.9	(6)
13	Cook	60	1.6	(9)
14	Presser	60	1.6	(11)
15	Butcher	59	1.6	(19)
16	Ice Dealer	55	1.5	(15)
17	Waiter	54	1.4	(10)
18	Printer	50	1.3	(23)
19	Bricklayer	46	1.2	(24)
20	Driver	46	1.2	(5)
21	Operator	43	1.1	(30)
22	Ice Man	41	1.1	*
23	Machinist	40	1.1	(8)
24	Plumber	33	.9	*
25	Electrician	31	.8	(33)
26	Cabinet Maker	22	.6	(35)
27	Upholsterer	20	.5	*
28	Grocer	19	.5	(28)
29	Fruit Dealer	18	.5	(18)
30	Fruit Store	18	.5	*
31	Laundry Worker	18	.5	*
32	Restaurant Worker	18	.5	*
33	Auto Mechanic	17	.5	*
34	Contractor	17	.5	*
35	Cutter	17	.5	*
36	Mason	17	.5	(25)
	All other occupations	1,415	33.2	
	Unknown	20	.5	

* Does not appear in leading occupations in Table III

LEADING OCCUPATIONS IN 1916 (Table III), WHICH DO NOT APPEAR IN LEADING OCCUPATIONS FOR 1931 (Table IV)

Rank in 1931	Occupation	Number	Per cent	Rank in Table III
40	Candy Maker	15	.4	(36)
49	Musician	13	.3	(27)
63	Longshoreman	10	.3	(20)
69	Cigar Maker	8	.2	(29)

Rank	Occupation	Number	Per cent	Rank in Table III
72	Hatter	8	.2	(34)
	Coal Dealer	0	0	(12)
	Piano Maker	0	0	(16)
	Bootblack	0	0	(31)
	Merchant	0	0	(32)

165

	TABLE V — OCCUPATIONS OF ITALIAN MALES, DECEASED IN NEW YORK CITY, 1916					TABLE VI — OCCUPATIONS OF ITALIAN MALES, DECEASED IN NEW YORK CITY, 1931			
Rank	Occupation	Number	Per cent	Rank in Table VI	Rank	Occupation	Number	Per cent	Rank in Table V
	Total	2,504	100.0			*Total*	3,778	100.0	
	36 *Leading Occupations*	1,663	62.5			36 *Leading Occupations*	2,488	65.0	
1	Laborer	658	22.3	(1)	1	Laborer	840	22.2	(1)
2	Student	233	9.3	(2)	2	Student	276	7.1	(2)
3	Barber	94	3.8	(4)	3	Tailor	134	3.5	(4)
4	Tailor	88	3.5	(3)	4	Barber	130	3.4	(3)
5	Longshoreman	44	1.8	(7)	5	Shoemaker	100	2.6	(7)
6	Driver	40	1.6	(28)	6	Carpenter	69	1.8	(9)
7	Shoemaker	38	1.5	(5)	7	Longshoreman	62	1.6	(5)
8	Shoe Worker	34	1.4	(15)	8	Painter	61	1.6	(11)
9	Carpenter	33	1.3	(6)	9	Chauffeur	56	1.5	*
10	Clerk	30	1.2	(10)	10	Clerk	55	1.5	(10)
11	Painter	28	1.1	(8)	11	Baker	50	1.3	(17)
12	Peddler	25	1.0	(13)	12	Salesman	50	1.3	(25)
13	Porter	22	.9	(16)	13	Peddler	43	1.1	(12)
14	Grocer	20	.8	(19)	14	Ice Man	37	1.0	*
15	Junk Dealer	20	.8	(30)	15	Shoe Worker	37	1.0	(8)
16	Merchant	19	.8	(40)	16	Porter	34	.9	(13)
17	Baker	18	.7	(11)	17	Cook	33	.9	(19)
18	Bootblack	16	.6	(18)	18	Bootblack	30	.8	(18)
19	Cook	16	.6	(17)	19	Grocer	28	.7	(14)
20	Waiter	15	.6	(36)	20	Bricklayer	27	.7	(21)
21	Bricklayer	14	.6	(20)	21	Printer	27	.7	(24)
22	Janitor	13	.5	(50)	22	Plasterer	26	.7	*
23	Mason	13	.5	(35)	23	Fruit Dealer	23	.6	(31)
24	Printer	13	.5	(21)	24	Butcher	22	.6	(29)
25	Salesman	13	.5	(12)	25	Musician	22	.6	(28)
26	House Worker	12	.5	(46)	26	Helper	21	.6	*
27	Machinist	11	.4	(31)	27	Contractor	19	.5	*
28	Musician	11	.4	(25)	28	Driver	19	.5	(6)
29	Butcher	10	.4	(24)	29	Watchman	19	.5	(34)
30	Fruit Dealer	10	.4	(23)	30	Junk Dealer	18	.5	(15)
31	Bartender	9	.4	(167)	31	Machinist	18	.5	(27)
32	Jeweler	9	.4	(51)	32	Mechanic	18	.5	*
33	Proprietor	9	.4	(33)	33	Proprietor	18	.5	(33)
34	Watchman	9	.4	(29)	34	Cabinet Maker	17	.4	*
35	Blacksmith	8	.3	(49)	35	Mason	17	.4	(23)
36	Cigar Maker	8	.3	(54)	36	Waiter	17	.4	(20)

All other occupations	416	20.5	All other occupations	801	22.1
Unknown	365	14.6	Retired	268	7.1
Retired	60	2.4	Unknown	221	5.8

* *Does not appear in leading occupation in Table* v.

LEADING OCCUPATIONS IN 1916 (Table V), WHICH DO NOT APPEAR IN LEADING OCCUPATIONS FOR 1931 (Table VI)

Rank in 1931	Occupation	Number	Per cent	Rank in Table V	Rank	Occupation	Number	Per cent	Rank in Table VI
40	Merchant	16	.4	(16)	50	Janitor	12	.3	(22)
46	House Worker	13	.3	(26)	51	Jeweler	12	.3	(32)
49	Blacksmith	12	.3	(35)	54	Cigar Maker	9	.2	(36)
					167	Bartender	1	—	(31)

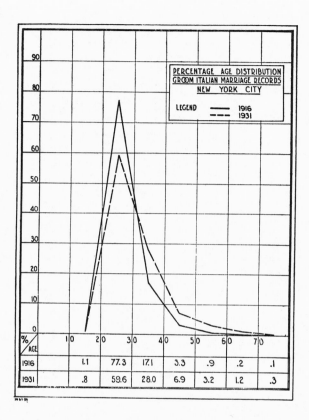

	AGE							
1916	1.1	77.3	17.1	3.3	.9	.2	.1
1931	.8	59.6	28.0	6.9	3.2	1.2	.3

TABLE IX

PERCENTAL TREND IN CONCENTRATION IN LEADING OCCUPATIONS OF ITALIANS IN N. Y. C.

	From Birth Records				From Marriage Records				From Death Records			
	1916		1931		1916		1931		1916		1931	
	%	Cumulative %	%	Cumulative %	%	Cumulative %	%	Cumulative %	%	Cumulative %	%	Cumulative %
5 leading occupations	66.1	66.1	47.9	47.9	50.2	50.2	28.0	28.0	40.7	40.7	38.8	38.8
Next 5 occupations	6.4	72.5	10.9	58.8	8.1	58.3	12.4	40.4	7.0	47.7	8.0	46.8
Next 5 occupations	3.9	76.4	7.2	66.0	5.5	63.8	8.7	49.1	4.6	52.3	5.7	52.5
Next 21 occupations	9.8	86.2	14.5	80.5	13.6	77.4	17.2	66.3	10.2	62.5	12.5	65.0
All other occupations	13.0	99.2	18.4	98.9	17.8	95.2	33.2	99.5	20.5	83.0	22.1	87.1
Unknown	.8	100.0	.7	99.6	4.8	100.0	.5	100.0	14.6	97.6	5.8	92.9
Unemployed			.4	100.0								
Retired									2.4	100.0	7.1	100.0

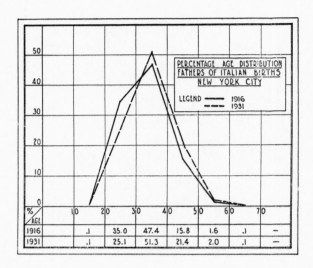

% / AGE	10	20	30	40	50	60	70
1916		.1	35.0	47.4	15.8	1.6	.1	—
1931		.1	25.1	51.3	21.4	2.0	.1	—

PERCENTAGE AGE DISTRIBUTION
FATHERS OF ITALIAN BIRTHS
NEW YORK CITY

LEGEND ——— 1916
- - - 1931

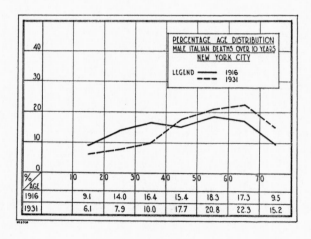

% / AGE	10	20	30	40	50	60	70
1916		9.1	14.0	16.4	15.4	18.3	17.3	9.5
1931		6.1	7.9	10.0	17.7	20.8	22.3	15.2

PERCENTAGE AGE DISTRIBUTION
MALE ITALIAN DEATHS OVER 10 YEARS
NEW YORK CITY

LEGEND ——— 1916
- - - 1931

CONCLUSIONS AND SUGGESTIONS
FOR FURTHER STUDY

It has often been asserted that the newer immigrants have inferior intelligence, figure more prominently in crime, and in general present greater social problems than the older stocks who immigrated to this country prior to 1880. Careful studies of the occupational trends of these ethnic groups may contribute to a clearer understanding as to the truth of such assertions. For example, if intelligence *as measured by our tests*, is a result of, rather than a cause of, differential levels in occupations, then the trend of an ethnic group from occupations of a lower level to a higher level should also show an increase in the general "intelligence" level for that group. The examination of such an assumption would, of course, require the carrying out of a testing program on a scale commensurate with that carried out in the last war.

This investigation, despite the limitations, indicates clearly that the distribution of Italians in the occupations is by no means static. Significant is the percental decrease in the classification of laborers. On the other hand, there is a definite increase in the diversification of leading occupations engaged in.

Both in 1916 and 1931, the following six occupations appear among the first fifteen, as shown in all six series:—Laborers, Tailors, Barbers, Shoemakers, Carpenters, Painters.

In 1931, four new occupations appeared among the first fifteen in all three lists:— Chauffeur, Clerk, Salesman, Baker.

Three others appeared on the two most significant lists:— Mechanic, Plasterer, Butcher.

It seems reasonable to conclude that this is an indication of a definite tendency for Italians to follow the occupational pattern set by the total population in New York City as reported in the U. S. Census of 1930.

This investigation has, it may be hoped, added somewhat to the common fund of knowledge relating to the occupational activities of the Italian immigrant population in New York City. It has set forth a considerable body of data from which certain generalization might be tentatively drawn and certain tendencies traced. Furthermore, some of the results of this and similar studies may be of direct use to the many social agencies working with immigrant groups. Such material, for example, as that relating to the number of workers in an occupation, and the changing distribution of the leading occupations, might well be taken into account in determining the social agencies' attitude toward their clients as regards programs for guidance in educational and occcupational fields.

Nevertheless, neither this nor any other study provides the material for a fully rounded guidance policy. For such a policy would, necessarily, have to rest on the answers to a series of questions which cannot be answered on the basis of existing data. What are the conditions that affect vocational choices? Which are environmental? How may we learn more of social status of an occupation? How may we determine the intelligence status of workers? These are some of the questions the answers to which may furnish the basis for a well-rounded social guidance program. Anything approaching adequate answers to these queries can not be derived from this study. Most of these topics must wait upon more extensive enumerations and more thorough analyses than have yet been completed.

The present fund of statistical information relating to occupations—extensive as it is—cannot therefore, be accepted as in any way providing an adequate statistical background for a well-rounded occupational program. It furnishes certain material, however, that may be of use in formulating a program. But it derives perhaps its greatest value from the fact that it calls attention to the importance of the problems; that it indicates the questions that must be elicited, the inadequacy of the present materials, and the need for a unified and coordinated plan; and that it suggests the paths that may be followed in seeking to answer these problems.

INDEX

INDEX

References are to entry numbers

About the author

Francesco Cordasco received his B.A. (Sociology) from Columbia College, Columbia University; his M.A. and Ph.D. from New York University; with postdoctoral studies at the London School of Economics, and at the Institute of Education, University of London. Presently, he is Professor of Educational Sociology at Montclair State College, and has taught at New York University, the City University of New York, and the University of Puerto Rico. He has served as a consultant to the Migration Division, Commonwealth of Puerto Rico; to the U.S. Office of Education; and to federal, state, and community antipoverty programs.

Professor Cordasco has published numerous articles and reviews in professional journals, and is the author of books on ethnicity and social class stratification in American education; on educational sociology; and on urban education and the immigrant child. His most recent book is *The Italians: Social Backgrounds of an American Group* (1974).

A Fellow of the American Sociological Association, and a Fellow of the British Sociological Association, Professor Cordasco is a native of New York City.